God Nods

GOD NODS

DISCOVER THE GREATEST TREASURE AT WORK

JOEY FAUCETTE
JANE CRESWELL

NASHVILLE

NEW YORK • LONDON • MELBOURNE • VANCOUVER

God Nods

Discover the Greatest Treasure at Work

© 2022 Listen to Life, Too

Published in New York, New York, by Morgan James Publishing. Morgan James is a trademark of Morgan James, LLC. www.MorganJamesPublishing.com

Proudly distributed by Ingram Publisher Services.

Publisher's Note: This novel is a work of fiction. Names, characters, places, and incidents are either products of the author's imagination or used fictitiously. All characters are fictional, and any similarity to people living or dead is purely coincidental.

Unless otherwise indicated, all Scripture quotations are taken from *THE MESSAGE*, copyright © 1993, 2002, 2018 by Eugene H. Peterson. Used by permission of NavPress. All rights reserved. Represented by Tyndale House Publishers, Inc.
Verses marked KJV are from the King James Version of the Bible.
Verses from the Amplified Bible are used with permission from The Lockman Foundation, http://www.lockman.org. Copyright © 2015 by The Lockman Foundation, La Habra, CA 90631. All rights reserved.

Morgan James BOGO™

A **FREE** ebook edition is available for you or a friend with the purchase of this print book.

CLEARLY SIGN YOUR NAME ABOVE

Instructions to claim your free ebook edition:
1. Visit MorganJamesBOGO.com
2. Sign your name CLEARLY in the space above
3. Complete the form and submit a photo of this entire page
4. You or your friend can download the ebook to your preferred device

ISBN 9781631955822 paperback
ISBN 9781631955839 ebook
Library of Congress Control Number:
2021935597

Cover Design by:
Jeremy Clark

Interior Design by:
Christopher Kirk
www.GFSstudio.com

Morgan James is a proud partner of Habitat for Humanity Peninsula and Greater Williamsburg. Partners in building since 2006.

Get involved today! Visit MorganJamesPublishing.com/giving-back

To our friend Judi Hayes
who kept telling us we needed to meet
because we talk about the same things.

CONTENTS

PREFACE

Work matters to God.

Your work, in fact.

The people you work with also matter to God

The customers or clients, vendors or suppliers you work with matter to God, too.

The mission of the company you work for and how you achieve it matter to God.

Your work matters to God.

So often we regard work as an east-of-Eden activity only. Work is the result of our fall from grace.

Sure, work got harder after our fall. And yet if you read Scripture carefully, you discover God employed the first man in the garden. Genesis 2:15 reads, "God took the Man and set him down in the Garden of Eden to work the ground and keep it in order."

In the original language, the word for "work" here later means "worship."

Work is worship.

Maybe you've heard that before. Or not.

Either way it's important because it means your work is significant to God. It's worship. And unless you work in a church facility, you worship outside of the walls of a church building, spaces like a home office or manufacturing facility or wherever else you get work done.

You worship God as you work.

Your work is your worship.

Not in a church, but as the church.

Believers worship Jesus, right?

Jesus works with you as you worship.

Matthew 18:20 has Jesus saying, "And when two or three of you are together because of me, you can be sure that I'll be there."

God is present through Jesus at work with you.

Sometimes you see God at work through Jesus.

That's a God Nod.

And that's what this little story is all about.

A couple of things to keep in mind as you read:

First, we scattered Scripture and coaching questions throughout the story in boxes. Yes, you're free to ignore them. And yet, to keep the story going so it becomes your story, take a moment to at least think about the question or activity.

Or grow your story as you join the larger Story—what God is doing through the God Nod movement—by using the QR codes in each box. These QR codes transform this book in whatever form you're consuming it into a Learning eXperience Book (LXB). In this online platform, you join other readers in the God Nod Community. You can answer the questions and do the activities in lots of ways like writing text or recording and uploading your own video just as you do on social media. You can react to and comment on one another's posts. You can do pretty much anything you do on social media. (Just be nice, OK?)

Also you'll find in the LXB opportunities to know us better. We post regular video interviews about the book and faith and work matters. And who knows? You may even discover more about some of the characters. Especially Lemondrop and . . . oh well. We'll avoid the need for spoiler alerts.

Be sure to return to the LXB even after you finish your first read through this little story as we host Zoom parties where you get to ask questions about the characters and your own faith and work matters. We talk about alternative endings, what the characters could do next—pretty much whatever you want to chat about. And readers are always adding new content about how God nodded at them recently. A lot of inspiration and encouragement are required to work in faith and look for God Nods today. The God Nod LXB is where you get it. And the God Nod LXB is yours free with this book purchase.

When you're ready to learn from the resources the characters use like their Faith Positive Fellowship Resources, you'll see where you can do that in the LXB. Yours is called God Nods Resources. Invite your coworkers to join you. Or start your own Fellowship among other believers who do what you do for work. What if human resources directors aka directors of people development like Abigail get together from around the world to learn from one another about what it means to believe in God Nods? Pretty exciting stuff, eh?

Here's what you do to join the God Nod Community:

1. Scan the QR code.
2. Complete the registration form which enrolls you.
3. Check your email for how to set up your password.
4. Log in and enjoy! (Yes, it's that easy.)

Be sure to log in from whatever devices you wish to join the God Nod Community online. Otherwise, you'll get reminded to with future QR codes.

Second, this little story time hops. Yes, it's set in the future. We suspect a nearer future than most of us imagine now, and yet we leave you to decide how far out.

Scenes time hop back and forth so pay particular attention to each character's experiences instead of the sequence. Time the way we keep it—forty-hour workweeks—matters little to God. God measures time in experiences, especially those with eternal significance. That's when you experience a God Nod. Besides, all of the characters' experiences come together at one time in the end. Just keep reading.

Our prayer for you as you read this little story is that you discover the treasure of God's presence within you and your work. See you online soon!

BEFORE YOU BEGIN . . .

Join the God Nod Community online free.
Share what you learn with others
and discover more as you read this book.
Here's what you do:

1. Scan the QR code.
2. Complete the registration form which enrolls you.
3. Check your email for how to set up your password.
4. Log in and enjoy! (Yes, it's that easy.)

Chapter 1

THE TREASURE

Charlotte Wilson cleared her throat and adjusted her chair, flipped her hair, and took a deep breath. Of course she was nervous. This interview was her first with a billionaire entrepreneur with a PhD and an MD. Sure, she was the most popular anchor on TVNZ, but this was *the* Dr. Elijah Campbell, after all. *The* Dr. Elijah Campbell, owner of Taonga Technologies who cured COVID-19 and -21 and disrupted the vaccine industry. *The* Dr. Elijah Campbell, only child of Oliver who owned Campbell Mining, the largest gold and precious metal mining operation in New Zealand. *The* Dr. Elijah Campbell—or was it Dr. Dr.?—who, it was rumored, would soon announce cures for various cancers, maybe even during this interview. He promised good news when he accepted her offer.

He declined all of her previous interview invitations. And yet he accepted this one only two days ago. What was different now?

She looked down at her notes and read his CV again:

"BS from Oxford with double majors in molecular biology and computer programming.

Masters from Duke in biomedical sciences.

PhD from Nanyang Technological University in Singapore in nanotechnology.

MD from Duke with specialties in oncology/hematology and infectious diseases."

"What if I don't understand a word he says?" Charlotte feared. "What if he geeks out on me? I'll look foolish with the whole world watching."

She scanned the PR brief again:

"Located in The Institute for First in Flight Adventures, Research Triangle Park (RTP), NC, Taonga Technologies (T2) discovered the antigen white blood cells could release to destroy COVID-19. Programming nanoids and injecting them into white blood cells, Dr. Elijah Campbell and team discovered how to stimulate that antigen's release. After killing COVID-19 and now -21 viruses, the white blood cells self-destruct to avoid mutation and the attack of other cells. Taonga Technologies pioneered the process of removing a patient's own white blood cells, enriching them with the specific antigen-producing nanoids, then transfusing them back into the patient with no side effects. The patient's body heals itself. New life emerges from certain death."

"'New life emerges from certain death.' I can remember that," Charlotte thought.

"Now what's their mission statement again?" Charlotte wondered. "Here it is: 'We discover great treasures within.'"

"Ms. Wilson? I'm Elijah Campbell," a tall, gaunt man said, wearing a wisp of a Mona Lisa smile.

"Oh yes, of course, Dr. Campbell. I'm so sorry," she stammered while standing up. "I'm Charlotte Wilson, TVNZ. Thank you so much for coming. I didn't know you were here."

"I snuck in a back door," he said. His dark eyes searched hers, as if staring into her soul, finding her best, and with that smile, bringing it to light.

"I'm a bit tired," he said. "I've just come from a wedding in the U.S. a week ago, and I'm not quite recovered. It was a most miraculous experience," his voice stopped to remember.

"May I sit down?" he managed.

"Oh yes," Charlotte said. "Of course."

And as *the* Dr. Elijah Campbell sat, Charlotte Wilson forgot how nervous she was and realized how peaceful she felt. Relaxed even, despite being in the presence of a billionaire entrepreneur with two doctorates. Maybe she could do this impossible interview after all.

Consider How God Nods at You

Read Mark 9:21-24. Recall a work experience when something that seemed impossible became doable. Like the boy's father, how did Jesus remove your disbelief? How might you approach doing the impossible better moving forward because of this experience?

"Charlotte, we're rolling," the producer said in her ear.

"Dr. Campbell," Charlotte began. "Thank you so much for taking time to chat with TVNZ and me. I'm quite privileged."

"Oh please call me Elijah," he said. There was that smile again. And those penetrating eyes . . . as if he saw something in her no one else did.

"OK Elijah," she said. "Tell us about the name of your company, Taonga Technologies. Why this name?"

"Oh Charlotte," Elijah said. "Thank you for asking that question. I now understand more about that name than ever before."

"How so?" Charlotte asked.

"Well, my earliest memories are of my father, Oliver Campbell, pulling me up into his lap, drawing me close enough to feel his warm breath on my face, and saying, 'Elijah, I discovered great treasures from the earth. You must go discover great treasures within,' and he would tap my chest right here."

"Well, you have made some great discoveries," Charlotte said.

"We have stumbled across some great treasures, this is true," Elijah said. "*Taonga* means 'natural treasure' in our native language. The implication is of war booty; to the victor go the spoils. This 'natural treasure' exists within us despite the war within."

"What does this natural treasure have to do with your medical accomplishments, Dr. Campbell?" Charlotte asked.

"Elijah," he said gently. "Charlotte, the human body is a natural treasure. We simply unlock the body's own natural abilities to defeat the rogue, invader cells who go to war. The spoils go to the victor—a healthy, healed body. And yet there's so much more. . . ." His voice trailed off again, like it just stumbled on another precious jewel of wisdom. "'Taonga' describes the great treasures within of which my father spoke . . ."

"And yet the company is named Taonga Technologies. What of the technologies?" Charlotte said.

"Yes, my father had great earth-moving machines that dug in the earth to find gold and precious metals. I knew I needed help in discovering taonga within the human body. That's when, as I studied in Singapore and Durham, I found nanoids could live within our white blood cells and prompt the release of specific, natural antigens to fight COVID-19, now COVID-21, and I believe other diseases as well. We held the key within all along. We just needed help releasing it at the proper moment to defeat the enemy. The nanoids could be programmed to prompt natural healing. Charlotte," Elijah said jumping up from his chair, reenergized. "We have everything we need to win the war. We just need help unearthing it. Like my father finding gold, only this great treasure was within, just as he said. So of course the company name is Taonga Technologies. Father was right. The greatest discovery of treasure is within," and with that Elijah slumped back into his chair.

Consider How God Nods at You

Read 2 Timothy 1:5-7. The apostle Paul (mentor), Lois (grandmother), and Eunice (mother) see Timothy's potential and encourage him. Who spoke great truth into your life at an early age? What truth did they speak that you understand better today?

Discover more about the characters
and places you met in this chapter.

Chapter 2
THE PROBLEM

Harper's Slack message popped up: "Hey Abby, got a minute?"

Abigail smiled and paused before responding. Harper's message could mean only one thing: another people problem.

Harper moved to Cary when Elijah Campbell started Taonga Technologies. It took a great deal of persuading for her and Noah to move from Island Bay, a suburb of Wellington in New Zealand, but Elijah usually gets what he wants. As the director of product development, Harper was brilliant in all things nanoids and coding. She and Elijah met as grad students in Singapore. But as her husband, Noah, often said, "Harper still thinks you can code people."

Abigail typed back, "Sure," and within seconds she heard a knock on her door.

"Come . . ." she started when Harper burst in.

"Abby, I'm so glad you're director of people development around here because if it was up to me, I'd fire about half of these folks and furlough the rest." And with that, Harper fell into an open chair.

"Well hello Harper. How are you today?" Abigail asked. "How are Noah and Ernie?"

"What?" Harper said. "Oh they're fine. I'm not here about them. It's Carl."

Carl, along with Akorfa, was Harper's lead coder. Another intellectually brilliant yet socially challenged technogeek whom Harper failed to code to her standards.

"Well how is Carl then?" Abigail said.

"He's about to die a slow, painful death. You'd better pray for him, Abby," Harper replied.

Abigail smiled and thought, *She asked me to pray. She brought up "prayer" first. So it's permissible for me to talk about prayer, . . . or is it? I'll just ask a question.*

"Have you prayed for Carl, Harper?" Abigail said.

"God and I aren't on speaking terms," Harper said. "I quit going to church and nobody noticed so I figured God quit caring when I quit going."

"Why did you quit going?" Abigail asked.

"The pastor said one Sunday that Sarah Young is a false teacher and *Jesus Calling* isn't worth the paper it's printed on. I haven't been back since. But no one noticed so I'm OK," Harper said.

"You don't sound OK," Abigail said. "You quit praying because of that?"

"Well Abby," Harper said, "*Jesus Calling* got me through our first year here in the States. And if that isn't true, I guess prayer isn't either. So, what good would it do for me to pray for Carl?"

Abigail smiled and thought, *Oh boy! Now she's going there. How far do I follow her into this rabbit hole of prayer? J. W. told me to go slow on Jesus conversations or else I'm on thin legal ice.*

Abigail inhaled slowly and said, "Well, I like *Jesus Calling*. In fact, I've read all of Sarah Young's books and I pray."

"Well, you better pray for Carl," Harper said, "because Sally is about to become a widow."

Abigail asked, "And what should I pray for?"

Consider How God Nods at You

Read Ephesians 6:18 in *The Message* translation of the Bible. Remember an experience when a coworker asked you to pray for someone difficult, even an enemy. How did you respond knowing, like Abigail, that you could be on "thin legal ice"? What did they want you to pray for? What would a "keep each other's spirits up" prayer sound like when praying for difficult people?

"Well," Harper said, "I don't really know what to pray for."

Abigail said, "If prayer doesn't work for you, what makes you think it'll work for me?" and then thought, *Lord knows I've prayed plenty of times and heard only crickets.*

"You go to church, right?" Harper said.

"Well, I used to before COVID-26, before the government shut the church doors," Abigail said.

"I thought they were opening back up now that we discovered the cure for the COVIDs," Harper said. "I just assumed everyone returned . . . including you. Everyone except me, that is."

"Not exactly," Abigail confessed and thought, *Now she's talking about church. Prayer and church! OK, she brought up both of these topics, not me. So I can respond to her prompts. Is that right? Oh, I wish I could remember exactly what J. W. said. We can't afford the loss of income if I violate some HR law even if it's in ignorance. And who knows what Harper could do? She's so impetuous.*

Harper said, "Hello, Abby? You in there?"

"Oh yea," Abigail replied. "I'm here."

"I just said I assumed you returned to church along with everyone else except me," Harper said.

I'm going for it since she brought up prayer and church, Abigail thought and then said, "I've gone to the recording sessions when I sing for worship. But I don't have to go to a building to pray, Harper, regardless of what a well-intended but misguided preacher like yours might say. I can pray right here, Harper, and so can you!"

Stand by, Abigail thought. *We're about to discover if I went too far.*

"Well, I don't know about that," Harper said. "God doesn't care to hear from me."

OK it's game on now, Abigail thought. *She's leading this conversation. I'm simply responding.*

"Harper, you're an amazing person whom God loves deeply," Abigail said. "Of course God cares."

"If God cares so much about me, why doesn't Carl get fixed?" Harper said.

Consider How God Nods at You

Share an experience when you prayed for someone and they failed to get fixed. How did it shape what you believe about prayer?

Great question, Abigail thought to herself.

She had wondered something similar since Sunday. Pastor Evangeline shared a message about how, since COVID-19, the church was transforming to more closely align with its created purpose to share God's love in Christ with the world. The temptation to huddle up inside a building morphed as fewer and fewer believers defied government orders following COVID-21 and instead worshipped in their homes. She said that's the way the first church gathered and then shared Christ's love as they worked and lived in a community. "All you need," she said, "is to gather at home or work, in person or virtually, with one or two of your neighbors or coworkers, and Christ is with you."

Abigail had read, even meditated over the Scripture she used—Matthew 18:18–20—especially the last verse, "And when two or three of you are together because of me, you can be sure that I'll be there."

Who are my two? she wondered. *Are my coworkers even aware that I know Jesus? And how do I let them know without violating any HR laws?*

Consider How God Nods at You

Read Matthew 18:18–20. How might your coworkers know you're a believer?

Abigail's answer sat right in front of her.

Harper knew. That's why she initiated this conversation.

She knew and waited impatiently for an answer to the God question about fixing Carl.

Abigail had her God Nod. She and a church quitter were the first two to gather. A couple of misfit believers—one of whom isn't even sure she believes—trying to figure out what it means to follow Jesus especially at work.

The church, such as it is, is planted at Taonga Technologies, Abigail mused to herself. *Wonder if this is what Jesus had in mind?*

Consider How God Nods at You

Read Matthew 16:17–18. The apostle Peter was a "misfit" similar to how Abigail and Harper see themselves. He almost drowned trying to walk on water. He cut off a soldier's ear. Three times he denied knowing Jesus. Yet Jesus declares he's building the church on Peter, whom he calls "the Rock." How does knowing this about Peter impact your understanding of how Jesus sees you and two or three of your coworkers? How could it transform the way you work?

Discover more about the characters
and places you met in this chapter.

Chapter 3

THE PRAYER

"**A**re you listening to me?" said Harper. "You keep zoning out on me. Are you OK?"

"I'm so sorry, Harper," Abigail replied, "I'm trying to figure out how much of this conversation I'm allowed to have with you based on, you know, current HR laws."

"Oh," Harper said, "I hadn't thought about that. And I really don't care. I just want to know if God cares so much about me, why doesn't Carl get fixed?"

"Good enough then," Abigail said. "I was also just thinking about you and me and what we could do for T2."

"What do you mean?" Harper asked.

"Well, take Carl for instance," Abigail said. "We've tried everything we can think of to help Carl. None of it's worked. What if we asked God to show us what to do?"

"I'm pretty sure God's frustrated with Carl, too," Harper said.

"Yea, well, I'm pretty sure God feels the same about me from time to time," Abigail said. "Yet here we are."

"I know God wishes I'd do better," Harper said, her voice softening.

Abigail asked Harper, "What was it about *Jesus Calling* that got you through the transition to life here in the U.S.?"

"It was like Jesus was talking directly to me," Harper said. "Like he loves me no matter how much I screw up, and like he is with—beside me, wherever I go."

"It's like God is present all the time," Abigail said, understanding what Harper said. "Feels kind of like that to me right now as we're sitting here talking," she offered.

"I'm glad it does for you," Harper said, "but I'm not so sure about me."

"Fair enough," Abigail said. "What do you remember about the last time you felt that close to Jesus?"

Harper sat quietly. Her eyes looked far beyond Abigail's spacious office. The afternoon sun peeked from behind a dark cloud and snuck in through the westward-facing window. She opened her mouth to speak, thought better, and pursed her lips. Then she exclaimed, "Well Abby, the only one I can think of is right after I stopped going to church when Noah came home with Ernie."

"Where was Jesus in that?" Abigail asked.

Harper smiled and spoke quickly. "At first I didn't see him. I just thought Noah was crazy. You know, being Noah again, getting his heart out in front of his head. And then I looked in that little boy's eyes, and Abby, I could have sworn I saw Jesus."

Abigail rubbed her right arm with her left hand. "You're giving me goose bumps," she said.

"Goose what?" Harper asked.

"Oh nothing," Abigail said. "It's just something I learned growing up in Georgia. What did Jesus look like?"

"He looked like . . . Ernie," she said. "That little guy smiled nervously at me, like he wasn't sure what was going on. Like he was trying to read my face or something. He stared into my eyes, and that's when I saw Jesus. At least I thought I did."

"What happened next?" Abigail asked.

"I heard myself saying to Noah, 'Of course, he can stay,'" Harper said. "And Abby, that's not even close to what I was thinking at first. But I said it anyway. And when I did, the kid smiled back at me, bigger this time, and I remember thinking, *This scared child needs me. He's one of the least of these.*" Harper dropped her head and dabbed at her right eye.

Consider How God Nods at You

Read Matthew 25:31-45. When have you seen Jesus among the least of these?

By now the sun had emerged completely from behind the cloud. Its warmth filled the office, completely immersing Harper's side.

Abigail sat dumbstruck. How could this impetuous, brilliant woman transform so quickly?

"And that's when I decided that maybe Sarah Young was right despite what the minister said," Harper continued. "Jesus is with me everywhere and every time. But I just couldn't bring myself to talk to God about my confusion and hurt."

The sun struck the corner of Abigail's desk. She said, "Harper, that's about as close as anybody could ever get to Jesus. And it happened in your home instead of a church service."

"You know," Harper said, "it really did. I felt a lot closer to Jesus there than in the last church service I went to. Really more than most of the services I've been in. What's up with that?"

"Jesus promised to be with us whenever two or more of us get together in his name," Abigail said. "So I guess Jesus was with you, Noah, and Ernie that day. And I wonder if he's up to something right here at work."

"I wish Carl could get some Jesus," Harper said. "Maybe he'd get fixed."

"Well," Abigail started, "how can we get some Jesus to Carl? We could pray for him like you said."

"That's your department, remember?" Harper replied. "The Big Guy and I aren't exactly on speaking terms."

"All right then," Abigail said. "I'll pray and you listen. Ready?"

"I guess so. Just not too long, OK? I've got some more work to do," Harper said.

Abigail smirked. "You're the one who came to see me and interrupted my work to talk about prayer and church."

"And Jesus," Harper said, "Yea, you're right. OK pray."

Abigail started, "Jesus, Harper and I are here today, the two of us, and we're asking you to help us with Carl. We've tried everything we know to do to help him, and Harper's really frustrated with him. We need Carl to do his best nanoid coding so we can cure pancreatic cancer and discover the treasure within. Show us how best to support Carl in his work. Amen."

Abigail looked up, and Harper's head was still bowed as she wiped more tears. The two sat in silence again. Finally, Harper spoke.

"I haven't really been supporting Carl," she said. "I've been pushing him to hurry up and telling him how disappointed I am in him—how slow he is. Kind of hard to get some Jesus to him like that."

"So, what can you do differently?" Abigail asked.

"I need some more Jesus myself," Harper said. "Isla is on my back constantly about the urgency to finish. 'People are dying daily from pancreatic cancer,' she says. Because of her actions, all I see is the negative in Carl. Jesus loves him, too. Unfortunately, I haven't."

The two sat in more silence, the reality of Harper's new awareness hung heavy in the room.

Harper continued. "I guess God created Carl just like he created us, huh?"

"Seems like it," Abigail replied.

The two of them relaxed into this different reality.

"So, what will you do now?" Abigail asked Harper.

"Since you asked Jesus to show us how best to support Carl, I guess that's what I've got to do," Harper replied. "After all, Carl belongs to God no matter how much I want to kill him at times. I'll start by telling him what I appreciate about his work. And ask how I can support him to do more of his best. And if he doesn't faint or have a heart attack, we'll just go from there and see what happens."

Harper jumped up to leave as abruptly as she entered and then stopped in the doorway.

"Thanks for listening," she said, "and for praying. It's been a while since I was that close to Jesus."

"Let's do it again sometime soon," Abigail said. "And we don't have to wait until Carl acts out. In fact, let me know how it goes with him. I hope you don't have to call Emergency Services," she laughed.

"Yea, me too," Harper said. "Pray for him," she said with a laugh, paused, and then more softly, "and me, too."

Consider How God Nods at You

Read Philippians 4:6 in *The Message*. What is one work worry you have right now that you could pray and petition God about? Who's someone at work that could pray with you?

Discover more about the characters and places you met in this chapter.

Chapter 4

THE BREAKDOWN

Josh sat outside Abigail's office, waiting for her to call him in.

Why am I always so early? he asked himself. *I just sit here and make myself nervous. I do it all the time. Well, I didn't know exactly how long their bioscanner would take.*

"Good day, friend!" Harper said.

"Oh, hello," Josh said and stood quickly, flashing his winsome smile. "I'm Josh. You must be Abigail. I'm delighted to meet you."

"Oh no. I'm Harper, director of product development. Abby does people development. I have yet to code a single person, although my husband, Noah, may disagree," and Harper laughed. Josh joined her.

Three weeks had passed since she and Abigail prayed together. Finally she had chatted with Carl. She hoped to surprise Abigail with an update from yesterday, but obviously she had an appointment with this fellow with the nice smile.

"Oh, I'm so sorry, Harper. I just assumed . . ."

"No worries," Harper said. "I'll make sure Abby knows you're here. Great to meet you, Josh. By the way, what brings you here?"

"I'm interviewing for the business development position," Josh said.

"Oh we definitely could use you," Harper smiled. "I'll let Abby know you're waiting," and she sauntered down the hall.

I heard Kiwis were friendly, Josh thought. *I'm definitely not in New York.*

One knock later Harper sat in front of Abigail as she finished up a Zoom call.

Abigail waved goodbye, closed her laptop, and said to Harper, "And do you need a review of the company privacy policy?"

"Well, you said last time we were together that since there were two of us, Jesus was here," Harper explained. "So I just popped in so Jesus would be with you. By the way, who's that handsome bloke waiting for you? Josh?"

Abigail shook her head and said, "I'm not sure that's what Jesus meant, and yes, that's Josh, who's early for his interview."

"Well I say hire him," Harper said, "and I came to tell you about Carl. I think God hears my prayers and cares about me after all!"

"Technically I did the praying," Abigail said with a smile.

"Yea, but I've been praying since then," Harper said. "Took me three weeks of praying just to get up the nerve to chat with him."

"OK, you have three minutes to report," Abigail said. "Ready, set, go!"

Harper said, "Relax sis. I only need one. Turns out Carl does have God's image and likeness in him."

"And what does that mean?" Abigail asked.

"It means all those prayers changed my thinking about Carl. Looking for his mistakes was my familiar pattern. I changed the code in my brain to look for his strengths. Well, actually God changed my code," Harper said. "After all, 'embracing what God does for you is the best thing you can do for him.'"

Consider How God Nods at You

Read Romans 12:1-2 in *The Message*. How can you best embrace what God's doing for you at work right now? Even if it's unfamiliar to you?

"Oh my," Abigail exclaimed. "You've been praying *and* reading Scripture?"

"Yes I have," Harper said with satisfaction. "Found that one in a Sarah Young book."

"And you're sowing positive thoughts in the mornings?" Abigail couldn't believe what she was hearing.

"A whole garden of them," Harper said, "and writing in my Gratitude Diary each night."

Abigail sat stunned.

"What? You thought I wasn't reading that book, *Faith Positive in a Negative World*, you sent me? Come on now. Sounds like your faith needs increasing," Harper teased.

Discover more about the best-seller,
Faith Positive in a Negative World, **and
the Gratitude Diary here.**

"OK. OK. Josh is waiting. What happened with Carl?" Abigail asked. "What do you mean Carl does have God's image and likeness in him?"

"OK, so I sensed Jesus downloading this code: go to Carl and ask him, 'How can I best support you?'" Harper said. "So I did."

"How fast did the EMS crew arrive?" Abigail asked with a smile.

"Funny, are you?" Harper replied. "Actually it did take him a minute to recover. I don't think he believed me. He asked me to repeat myself. So I did."

"And what did he say?"

"I had no idea what he would say. I just knew what I was supposed to ask him," Harper said. "He looked down at his desk, and said, 'How did you know? I didn't want anyone to know.'"

"Know what?" Abigail said.

"That's what I said," Harper said. "Then he told me his grandson, Henry, who's about one, has a brain tumor and is undergoing massive chemo treatments in preparation for a stem cell transplant."

"What? That's horrible. Poor guy. No wonder he's unable to do his best work. What did you say?" Abigail said.

"I know, eh? I just thought he was being Carl again," Harper said. "So I asked again how I could best support him. And the guy broke down. Right there at his desk. Didn't care who was watching him. And I'm thinking, 'Jesus, I didn't sign up for this!'"

"OK, look. Josh is waiting. What did Carl say?" Abigail said.

"Well, he said he didn't know. And I'm like, 'I got nothing,'" and then Harper said, "but I asked him if we could pray for him. You and me. I told him we pray together. Like talk to Jesus and stuff, eh? I know I broke about a hundred HR rules, but I did it anyway. I said it before I thought."

Consider How God Nods at You

Read Romans 8:26-27. It's difficult to know how to pray for someone when they are unsure of their prayer request. How might these verses redefine your prayer strategy in such situations?

"And what did he say?" Abigail asked.

Harper said, "He said, 'I guess so, but I quit going to church so I'm not sure God cares about me anymore.'"

"What?" Abigail said.

"I know," Harper said. "It was like he was in my head a few weeks ago. I asked him what happened. He said his daughter wasn't married when Henry was born. The other moms at church didn't want them around. Said this brain cancer was God's judgment."

"Oh my word," Abigail said.

"I don't know if I did right or not, Abby, but I told him God loves Henry and his mom and Carl and Sally as much as he loves anybody in the world," Harper said quickly, "and that we would pray for his healing and for peace for the rest of them. I hope that was OK," and her voice trailed off as if asking a question.

"We'll know more later," Abigail replied. "But confidentially I would have done the same" and she opened her laptop, opened a file labeled "Prayers" and typed, "Carl's grandson, Henry, and family." Then she said, "Let's do lunch together and pray for them, OK?"

"And I'll pray you hire Josh. I like his spirit . . . and his smile!" Harper said as she jumped up to leave.

As Harper shut the door behind her, Abigail opened another file, "God Nods." She clicked on the folder, "Harper," dated the entry, and wrote, "Prays, reads Scripture, and does Gratitude Diary daily."

Consider How God Nods at You

Read 1 Thessalonians 5:16-18. What new habits could you adopt to "pray without ceasing" (1 Thessalonians 5:17, KJV) at work like Abigail?

Discover more about the characters
and places you met in this chapter.

Chapter 5
THE INTERVIEW

Harper walked by Josh, who was still seated, poked him in the arm, and said, "I put in a good word for you."

"Oh OK. Thanks!" Josh replied and then to himself, "I think . . ."

"I see you met Harper," Abigail said walking up to Josh. "You know how unique coders are, right?"

"Oh I sure do, Abigail," Josh shot back. "You are Abigail, aren't you? I mistook Harper for you earlier."

"It happens," Abigail said. "And please call me Abby. I'm the one with the better personality."

Josh laughed. "Thanks so much, Abby. I'll remember that the next time I see Harper."

"Come on in. Would you like something to drink? Water? Coffee?" Abigail offered.

"I'm good," Josh replied. "Fully caffeinated and hydrated."

"Well then, have a seat and let's get to know each other," Abigail said.

And with that the two of them discovered more than the usual in a brief conversation. Josh had led business development for several California-based biomed companies. This Taonga Technologies opportunity intrigued him because he could expand into some operational responsibilities as well, more managing partnerships with medical school research centers and manufacturing and distribution interests than just big pharma-type sales. He had been there and done that. Had the receipts from thousands of lunches to prove it.

His partner, Mandy, recently took a new position at the Kittrell Heights School in Durham where she teaches seventh-grade math. He was tired of so much coast-to-coast travel—when he could—and liked the appeal of diversifying his skill set to more closely match his strengths. His intense desire to relocate from San Francisco to the Triangle area with Mandy made the position almost irresistible.

"But you realize you set your own schedule for coming into the office, right?" asked Abigail.

"Yes, I do. To be honest, the most important attraction factor for me in working with Taonga Technologies is your mission. I mean first of all, what company integrates medicine and technology better than you?" Josh said. "You're the leading biomedical technology company in the world, saving millions of lives from COVID-19 and -21 alone. Plus whose mission statement could be any better: to discover the treasure within? Its spiritual value speaks volumes."

"It really does," Abigail agreed. "This position sounds like more than a job for you."

"Yes, it is," Josh replied. "And it's more than a career move, too. I'm thinking of it as a calling."

"Hmmm," Abigail said. "That's interesting."

"Well, I hope you hear what I'm not saying," Josh said.

"I don't know what you mean," Abigail responded.

"This is kind of awkward," Josh said. "And I've never thought this way before. I think there's a greater purpose in my working for Taonga Technologies, but I don't know what it is. Really it's more a feeling than a thought. Something I've never felt before. Almost like I'm supposed to be here. Sorry. I know that sounds weird."

Consider How God Nods at You

Read Genesis 2:15. God put Adam to work as a part of his purpose. How would your work be different today if you embraced your work as your purpose? What changes could you make to embrace your purpose more?

"Oh," Abigail said and then, "Ooooohhh. I think I understand now. Thank you for your transparency."

"Well, I probably just lost any chance I had at this position, and I know that sounds really strange, and I've never said anything like that before, and I don't even know why I said it," the words tumbled from Josh's lips faster than he typically talks.

Abigail leaned forward in her chair toward Josh.

Looking up briefly, she smiled. Another God Nod.

"Josh," she said, "it's OK. I get it. When would you like to start?"

"What? Just like that?" Josh asked.

"Oh yes," Abigail replied, "just like that."

Thirty days later Josh unpacked the last box in his new home office, kissed Mandy good-bye as she headed to school, took a deep breath, and logged into his first Zoom meeting with Abigail.

Consider How God Nods at You

Read Isaiah 43:19–21. Remember an experience when God called you to something new at work. Describe the call experience and include your wows and woes. What did you let go of to embrace the "new thing"?

Discover more about the characters and places you met in this chapter.

Chapter 6
THE LEADER

Lunch found Abigail and Harper together again, heads bowed over natural nutrient shakes, asking God to heal Henry.

"I sure hope that helps," Harper said.

"Can't hurt," Abigail said. "Helps me to pray for others."

"Yea well, we'll see. Carl came back to me and apologized for oversharing about Henry. Said he'd get more productive quickly. Do his job better," Harper said.

"What did you say?" Abigail asked.

Harper replied, "I told him how much I admired his courage in sharing. That I knew he would get his work done. And that we were praying for Henry at lunch today."

"And?" Abigail asked.

"He said he knew Isla is on my back about this latest nanoid code to prompt the white blood cells to release the antigen to destroy the pancreatic cancer cells," Harper said. "I acknowledged she's pretty intense, but I could handle her. I know her daddy really well."

"Dr. Campbell's daughter can be a bit difficult at times," Abigail said.

"Aw, she's just intense. I, on the other hand, can be difficult at times," Harper laughed. "At least that's what Noah says, but what does he know? He married me."

Abigail asked, "What was Carl's response?"

"He thanked me," Harper said. "I asked how he's holding up. He said instead of staying home and drinking too much, he spent some time with Henry overnight, just the two of them, in the PICU. Said he had more peace than from drinking. Thanked me for praying. I told him it was our privilege."

"Wow," Abby said. "Who would have thought that?"

"What?" Harper asked.

"That you would respond to Carl like that," Abigail said, sipping on her shake.

Harper sat quietly, smiled at the table, and then looked up. "Yea, you know it's not me, right? It's Christ in me."

"I see Him in you," Abigail replied. "He looks good in you."

Consider How God Nods at You

Read Ephesians 1:11-12 in *The Message*. How do you see Christ in your coworkers? How do you recognize Christ in yourself at work?

"It's that image and likeness thing again," Harper said. "I don't understand the programming code. Really, I don't even know what language it's written in. But I can tell you it works. The more I start my mornings reading Scripture and praying and end my day with the Gratitude Diary, the more peace and calm I experience. It's really nice."

"Anybody besides Carl noticed?" Abigail asked.

"Akorfa. She talked with me the other day," Harper said, "about something she wanted to try. Frankly it was out of the blue. Not our typical scientific method process. I said, 'Sure. Give it a go.' She almost fainted right there on Zoom."

"What happened next?" Abigail said.

"She came back a day later and asked me if I was sure she could try it," Harper said. "I said I said yes. She said how much she appreciated the opportunity to try something out of the norm. Mentioned that she had a dream and this potential solution appeared to her. I said, 'Well, let's see if you've lost your mind or found it.'"

"Geez, Harper," Abigail said. "You know Akorfa lives in Ghana. She's one of the nicest people on the planet. Brilliant, too. What did she say? Did you offend her?"

"She laughed so hard she nearly fell into a worktable," Harper said. "I just told her the truth. When she stopped laughing, she thanked me for whatever it is I'm doing to grow as a leader. She celebrates the new me."

"Wow, Harper," Abigail said. "What was it like to hear that?"

"Kind of good. I thanked her and told her it was Jesus in me she liked better," Harper said.

"Oh goodness, Harper," Abigail said. "You've got to stop all of this Jesus talk!"

"Now come on, Abby," Harper said. "You're the one who prayed for all of these spiritual shenanigans. Besides, Akorfa took it in stride."

"What did she say?" Abigail asked.

Harper quietly replied, "She said, 'I know.'"

Abigail was unable to speak, her mouth agape. She thought, "Another God Nod!"

Consider How God Nods at You

Read 2 Corinthians 2:14–16 in *The Message*. What is your spiritual growth edge as a leader where your coworkers could notice "the exquisite fragrance" of Christ in you?

Chapter 7
THE FILTER

Abigail waved at Josh. "Good morning and welcome officially to Taonga Technologies!"

Josh waved back. "Thank you! And I so appreciate your letting me work from home on my first official day. Gave me the chance to make Mandy's favorite breakfast casserole of cheese grits with bacon. You can't buy grits in San Francisco."

Abigail laughed. "Glad to help out. My husband, J. W., still hasn't acquired a taste for grits. Being from the UK, he thinks grits should be sweet like hasty pudding."

"That's funny," Josh said. "Mandy grew up in the other Birmingham, as in Alabama, so she knows her grits."

"And now my breakfast protein shake sounds miserable," Abigail said. "So let's start your onboarding. Thanks for watching all of the videos and joining our T2 Learning Community. I see you met a lot of our team members."

"I did," said Josh. "That's a great learning experience platform you use. And the gaming development activities helped me get up to speed quickly. That's quite a story about Dr. Campbell's 'discover the treasures within' mission. When do I get to meet him?"

"Well," Abigail hesitated, "I'm not really sure. He's been rather reclusive lately."

"OK, well just know I'd love to when it's appropriate," Josh offered.

"Sure. Of course," Abigail replied. "You know that as a part of your onboarding, you receive coaching from me. So, what would you like to talk about today?"

"Yes, and I appreciate it," Josh said. "I understand that this includes mentor coaching also, right?"

"Absolutely," Abigail said.

"OK, well I need some mentor coaching because it seems like I've marched off my map," Josh said. "And Mandy isn't very helpful."

"All right then," Abigail said. "What's on your mind?"

"You remember how I told you that working for Taonga Technologies seems more like a calling for me? Something spiritual? But I can't explain it because I don't understand it?"

Abigail replied, "Yes, I do. It's one of the many reasons I hired you."

"OK, I thought so," Josh said. "And so I want you to know I searched you online before the interview."

"Oh really?" Abigail said. "You stalking me, Josh?"

"No, just searching to see who you really are," Josh said.

"Well, that's fine," Abigail laughed. "I stalked you before our interview, too!"

"I saw you," Josh laughed back. "So something I found on you had a lot to do with why I was comfortable saying 'calling' to you."

Abigail said, "Really? What was that?"

"I saw you singing. In a virtual worship service. At least it looked like you. And the description said it was you. It was you, right?"

"Depends," Abigail said. "What do you think you saw me singing?"

"Well, it was actually you and some other singers," Josh said. "I watched it about twelve times. The song was 'Love Theory.'"

"Oh yea, well that was definitely me," said Abigail. "I love some Kirk Franklin!"

"I get that! I found his music video of that same song," Josh said. "But look, what does the lyric mean, 'I don't wanna love nobody but you?' Who are you talking about?"

"You sure you want to go here, Josh?"

"Yes, because you're singing this song, and it keeps talking about Jesus. Every time I searched for 'calling' before our interview, I wound up at a listing for *Jesus Calling*, so I'm thinking there has to be some connection between my calling to Taonga Technologies and this Jesus. Am I making any sense whatsoever? 'Cause I got nothing," Josh said, his words stumbling over one another, mixed with fear and fascination.

Abigail sat quietly, her mind raced. *Another God Nod*, she thought, her heart pounding.

"OK Abby," Josh said. "I know this isn't what you had in mind for our first session so just forget I brought it up. I'm sorry. I bet you wish you hired someone else now."

"Oh no, Josh! The opposite is true," Abigail said. "I'm amazed you brought this connection up. So yes, that was me singing that song. Thanks for listening. And yes, I'm familiar with that book, *Jesus Calling*, but Harper is the one you should talk to about it."

"Harper? Really?" Josh asked.

"Yes, it's her favorite book," Abigail said. "Now what makes you think there's a connection between Jesus and your calling to work here?"

"I keep running into him every time I search 'calling,'" Josh said. "And then that song and the lyrics, 'I don't wanna love nobody but you.' Sounds like when you have a calling, you're all in with this Jesus, and I don't even know what that means. I just do business development. I love Mandy."

Consider How God Nods at You

Read 2 Peter 1:10-11 in *The Message*. How is your work a calling? What does it mean for you to "confirm God's invitation to you"?

"Well, Josh," Abigail said, "your calling is like a filter. Everything you think or say or do passes through this filter. When a thought or word or action at work complements your calling, it passes through. You think or say or do it. When it doesn't, you stop it at the filter."

"OK, but what about Jesus and my calling?" Josh asked. "What does it mean to be all in with Jesus at work? And why do I want to do that with Jesus of all people?"

"Who is Jesus to you, Josh?" Abigail asked.

Josh's head dropped in silence. Still looking down, he said, "Great question, and that's where Mandy was no help. I asked her if she knows anything about Jesus, and she gave me that look I get occasionally. That, 'Are you crazy?' expression that means she doesn't want to go there."

Abigail smiled big and said, "Yea J. W. gets that look more often than occasionally."

"I really don't know much at all about this Jesus," Josh said. "I just know he's connected to my calling here, and I want to understand more. Is there something I can read about him? There are so many conflicting blogs and videos online."

Consider How God Nods at You

Read Mark 8:27-29. Who is Jesus to you? And how will you explain who he is to someone unfamiliar with him?

"There is something to read to learn more about Jesus," Abigail said.

"Please don't say the Bible," Josh interrupted, "because I opened that book, read the first three chapters, and quit. It made no sense at all."

Abigail laughed again and said, "I know what you mean. There are other books in the Bible though that make a lot more sense. For instance, the book of John is really helpful in knowing who Jesus is."

"I guess I can try that one. I didn't get that far last time. Is it on audiobook?" Josh asked.

"Yes, it is," Abigail said. "Find it in *The Message* translation. That's my favorite."

"OK. What else can I do to connect this Jesus and my calling?" Josh said.

Abigail thought quickly and then said, "Do you mind if I see when Harper's available to join us? She has a story to tell you about her calling and Jesus."

Consider How God Nods at You

Read Ephesians 4:1-3 in *The Message*. What does it mean for you to be "all in with Jesus" at work? How can you explain it in three short sentences to someone who doesn't know what it means?

Discover more about the characters and places you met in this chapter.

Chapter 8
THE RESISTER

sla sat staring out the window. The gray day was atypical of North Carolina weather this time of year. The brilliant sun had faded, covered with storm clouds that promised only misery.

She joined Taonga Technologies as a fifteen-year-old. She helped code what became the building blocks for all of the nanoid programming. "You're brilliant," her Daddy used to say to her. "That's why I named you Isla."

That was the same year her mother died on an icy I-40 returning home to Cary from volunteering at Eastside Elementary School in Durham. Why her mother thought she could make a difference in those kids' lives was beyond reason. Certainly not something to give her life for.

Mother was the parent all of the other girls wanted as their own. Isla knew that . . . now. Her friends said as much as they chatted online after the virtual funeral. The government's

43

COVID-19 restrictions determined who could and could not come to the service. It was just as well with Isla. As an only child, she had no one to console her or any idea of how they could. Not even her daddy.

She finished her school year virtually at the North Carolina School of Math and Science. Not that she learned a lot. Her eidetic memory was her greatest asset and liability. While the teachers tried their best, none really challenged her under the best of conditions. Her mother's death and the deep grief that followed for months did little to lessen her memory's accuracy or capture her imagination.

The only outlet that made any sense at all to Isla was programming. The simplicity yet complexity of a world constructed only of zeros and ones was logical, rational, and controllable. Daily she finished her schoolwork by noon and then immersed herself in coding, as if her mother's spirit lay somewhere underneath the puzzle offered by nanoids, COVID-19, and a white blood cell antigen.

Her daddy found the antigen, and while he was highly skilled in nanotechnology and programming, he always said her fresh eyes, her hyper-focused attention, and her relentless perseverance were not his own and yet required to code the nanoids accurately.

When she found the code and presented it to him, she expected at least a smile. Instead, his sad eyes stared back while his blank mouth said, "Thank you." Even after further testing secured her code's accuracy and it was patented, "I'm proud of you" was the best he could muster. Mother's death was difficult for him, too.

Her reward for coding the nanoids to both stimulate the COVID-19's antigen release from white blood cells and then self-destruct so as not to mutate was her worst nightmare. First she lost her mother. Now she must lose her father.

He sent her away to another boarding school to finish her high school education. Away from home.

"Now don't get me wrong," she would say years later, "Chatham Hall is a most excellent school. I received an amazing education. But what I really needed was my daddy."

From Chatham Hall she continued her search for her daddy. She did her undergraduate work at Oxford with graduate work at Duke. Her only variation from his path was her PhD in nanotechnology was from the Hong Kong University of Science and Technology. Oh, and she didn't like people well enough to do an MD.

Thanks to tens of thousands of dollars in therapy, she could now say with confidence, "Daddy did the best he could." And yet it still wasn't enough.

Every little girl needs a daddy who cares.

As she stared back out the window, Isla noticed a faint hint of sun peeking through the miserable, gray day. *Probably won't last*, she thought and turned back to her struggle to build code from Harper's team's efforts around a cure for pancreatic cancer. She didn't have much time. Daddy grew weaker by the day.

Consider How God Nods at You

Read Psalm 23:4. Share as best you can some of your challenges walking "through Death Valley."

Chapter 9

THE FIRST-GATHERERS

Three mornings later, Abigail, Harper, and Josh sat quietly in Abby's office at 6:30. She read these words: "When two of you get together on anything at all on earth and make a prayer of it, my Father in heaven goes into action. And when two or three of you are together because of me, you can be sure that I'll be there" (Matt. 18:18–20)

"There are three of us here," Abigail said, "and it's because of Jesus and his calling that we're here. So I guess we can be sure he's here, too."

"Should I go get another chair?" Josh offered.

"Come on now, friend," Harper started.

"Actually," Abigail interrupted, "that's a great idea. Please do, Josh."

Harper looked at Abigail with her classic, "Have you lost your mind?" look. Abigail smiled back and whispered,

"I do people development. You do product development. I got this."

Josh plopped the chair down beside his own chair and said, "Is it OK if he sits beside me? I have some questions."

They all laughed a sudden, loud burst of nervous tension that ceased as quickly as it started, then settled into anxious silence. The reality of the moment and that empty chair settled on them, heavy at first, then strangely lighter.

Consider How God Nods at You

Read Matthew 18:18-20. Who might your "two or more" believers be with whom you could gather? What prevents you from gathering with them?

"I wanted the two of you to gather with me this morning because Harper has a powerful story to share and because Josh has a powerful question: What does it mean to be 'all in with Jesus,' especially at work?"

"That and," Josh said, "what does this sense of calling to work here have to do with Jesus? He keeps showing up in my searches."

Harper smiled and said, "I get that" and started her story with how she quit church and assumed God didn't care because no one else did. And then she talked about Carl, his sick grandson, and Carl's drinking and lack of good work. Isla's obsessive, daily pressure for a nanoid code to cure pancreatic cancer. Her and Abby's praying for Carl—the first prayer Harper sat in on in a long time. Of Harper seeing Carl for the first time as having the image and likeness of God within and how he responded when she asked how she could support him. How Akorfa noticed Harper's leadership developing beyond what she could control and how Akorfa experienced Christ in Harper. Harper finished her story by saying, "So Josh, I don't know if any of this helps you understand your calling and what Jesus has got to do with your working at T2, but it helps me know my work makes a difference and that I'm not working alone. Jesus is with me," and with that she pointed to the empty chair.

After a long moment, Josh said, "That's some story," and sat quietly, his brow furrowed yet his trademark smile emerging at his mouth's corners, almost out of habit. Forced yet free.

"Josh," Abigail said, "are you OK?"

Josh said, "Yea, I am. That's just some story."

"If it helps any, it sounds strange to me coming out of my mouth," Harper said. "I'm not exactly the religious type, you know."

Abigail said, "Josh, it is quite a story, and yet let's remember that it is Harper's story. We each can have our own stories about God's calling to be like Jesus at work."

"Well, I've been reading John's book in the Bible like you suggested," Josh said. "You're right. It makes a whole lot more sense than the beginning book."

"And?" Abigail asked.

"And," Josh said, "John's Jesus and Harper's Jesus sound a lot alike. He helped a lot of people just by asking questions and doing what they asked. Kind of like Harper did with Carl."

"Yea, but I think it came a little more naturally to Jesus," Harper said, and all three of them laughed out loud, a comfortable, relaxed "you got that right!" expression that wrapped it's arms around them and drew them closer.

"So, if Carl has God's image and likeness inside of him, I guess I do, too?" Josh asked.

Harper piped up. "Sure you do!"

"Well, that's good to know. And that's one thing I do remember reading from that beginning book in the Bible. What's it called?"

"Genesis," Abigail offered.

"Yea, that's it," Josh said. "God breathed into that first guy, and he came alive with the image and likeness of God in him."

Consider How God Nods at You

Read Genesis 1:26–27; 2:7 in The Amplified Bible. How are you created in the "image and likeness" of God? What about your coworkers? Boss? Customers? What impact does God's "image and likeness" have on how you work?

"I guess that's how Jesus can be here with us," Harper said, her voice rising with excitement.

"I like to think of Harper's experiences as just that: proof positive that Jesus works alongside us, helping us find our way and others, too," Abigail said. "I call them God Nods."

"I like that," Josh said. "God Nods."

"Yea," Harper said, "like Jesus is cheering us on, encouraging us, giving us joy at work."

"And helping you, Harper," Abigail said, "love God and others like Carl more."

"I need all the God Nods I can get then," Harper said with a smile.

Josh smiled again, full faced this time. "I get it now."

"Get what?" Abigail asked.

"'Discover the treasure within' is the T2 mission. The treasure is more than the body's natural antigens we help release that cure diseases. The treasure is Jesus is in here," Josh said as he tapped his chest. "We can code our work habits to release Jesus."

"And we code our work habits," Harper continued, "by looking for the God Nods."

"And when we do, it means Jesus works with us," Abigail said.

"Hey!" Josh jumped up. "That means Jesus does our business development!"

"And our product development!" Harper jumped up with him.

They both stared at Abigail who smiled, stood slowly, and said, "Well, of course Jesus is primarily in people development."

As all three of them stood and yet while no one was looking, Isla walked by and wondered almost out loud, *What are those three up to so early in the morning? And why are they standing?* She took a step in their direction, then shook her head, and instead headed down the hall to meet with Daddy.

Consider How God Nods at You

Read Matthew 28:20. Share one God Nod you've experienced recently at work. How did Jesus work with you?

Chapter 10
THE TEAM

Charlotte Wilson repositioned herself in her chair as Elijah Campbell slumped back into his. "That's all very exciting, Elijah," she said. "Now who makes these discoveries of the treasure within? Is it just you? You're quite a brilliant man."

Elijah sat up abruptly with a laugh that rang through the studio. He could hardly speak for laughing, "Is it just me?" he said.

Charlotte stammered through her fake smile. "Well, you are brilliant, sir," which only fueled Elijah's laughter, even louder this time.

"Oh goodness, Charlotte," Elijah managed. "You're quite the humorist." He looked at her pained expression and said, "I'm so sorry. I apologize. I have offended you."

"No, it's OK," Charlotte started.

Elijah interrupted, "Regardless of how brilliant you think I am, I am just a man. Discoveries of this magnitude require more than one. Teams of people work together from all over the world like a body. The eye sees, the brain thinks, the nerves carry signals, the muscles move so the hand grasps and the foot walks. We are one body at T2 all committed to discovering the treasure within . . . a body and treasure that far exceeds my wildest dreams, or so I found out recently."

"So, who are some of the parts of this body-team at T2?" Charlotte asked.

"OK, for example, my daughter Isla," Elijah began, "discovered the nanoid programming building blocks as a fifteen-year-old, the same year her Mother died, my dear sweet wife who knew more about life than I could ever hope to." His voice faded off again, as he remembered her. "Despite the pain of grief, Isla brought new life to millions out of certain death."

There's that memorable line, Charlotte thought and then said, "Is she still with T2 today? Isla, that is."

"Oh yes, of course. The doors stay open because of her," he said, "and are open even wider now, thank God."

"And others?" Charlotte asked.

"Oh, there are so many more with each one equally important. Harper, Abigail, Carl, Akorfa, and we just added Josh. We all regard one another highly and remain humble so we work together for mutual benefit to solve these great puzzles of the human body. We listen actively to one another. We put just enough pressure on one another to bring out the best in one another. Some call that accountability. And we treat one another as we wish to be treated," Elijah said.

Charlotte wondered out loud, "How did you create such a phenomenal culture?"

Elijah laughed out loud again, this time stopping himself before Charlotte grew uncomfortable. "That's the point, Charlotte. I didn't create such a phenomenal culture. We do. All of us work together, called out for this purpose of discovering the treasure within." He looked intently into Charlotte's clear blue eyes.

There are those eyes again, staring into my soul, Charlotte thought quickly. *He knows I'm thinking, "How can I join your team?"*

Consider How God Nods at You

Read 1 Corinthians 12. How does your company work as a body? What is your part in this body? How can you transform your company culture to work more body-like?

Chapter 11

THE INVITATION

Isla walked down the hall toward her daddy's office, wondering how he felt today.

Inside Abigail's office, she, Harper, and Josh decided to pray while they stood there. She led the prayer, asking for more God Nods to give direction; for Harper, Carl, and Akorfa to lead Taonga Technologies to discover the nanoid coding that would eliminate pancreatic cancer; and then for specific persons like Carl who struggled to find their way in their current adversity.

"And Jesus," Abigail prayed, "for some reason Isla is on my heart right now. I ask that she work more like you with Harper and her team. In fact, Father, please give us opportunities to show Isla Jesus. Amen."

Silence circled the room until Harper said, "Oh boy, now you've gone and done it."

"What?" Abigail asked.

"Isla. I'm not even sure Jesus can break down those walls," Harper answered.

"Speaking of breaking down walls," Josh said, "would you two and your husbands like to come over for dinner one evening? I keep asking Mandy if she knows about Jesus, and she just looks at me and calls me 'weird.' Maybe meeting some more weird people might help."

"I can ask J. W. when he's available," Abigail offered.

Harper responded, "I'm happy to tell Noah we're going" and laughed.

"OK great," Josh said. "Let me talk with Mandy and get back with you."

Consider How God Nods at You

Read 1 Peter 2:9. Share an experience when someone regarded you as "weird" because of your relationship with Jesus. How does your being "chosen by God" influence that label of "weird"?

Two weeks later, Abigail and J. W., along with Harper and Noah, were seated around Josh and Mandy's table.

"I'll go first," Noah said. "I'm a speech pathologist by calling with a certification in dyslexia. I work at Eastside Elementary School in Durham where I particularly enjoy helping dyslexic kids learn to read and process their learning. I was the program director for the school system, but I missed the interaction with the children so I went back into a school. Sophie Campbell was one of my volunteers early on until her death."

"Was she Dr. Campbell's wife?" Josh asked.

"Yes," said Abigail, "and Isla's mother."

"When she died in the car accident," Noah said, "I went into administration. I've healed now and was ready to get back into the classroom."

"Go ahead and tell them," Harper said.

"Tell them what?" Noah asked.

"So he goes back into the classrooms," Harper explained, "and one day, I'm working from home, coding my brains out, and in he walks with this kid holding his hand, and says, 'Sweetheart, meet Ernie. Ernie, this is my sweetheart, Harper.' I don't know who was more scared, Ernie or me!"

"Oh. That." Noah said. "Yea, well the backstory is his mum was arrested in a drug bust, and nobody came to pick him up from school. I told CPS we had an extra bedroom as they were full . . ."

"That was about a year ago, and we adopted Ernie last month," Harper said. "He's the cutest little bloke you've ever seen. Noah tutors him at home, and they have so much fun."

"He does have a bit of trouble with our Kiwi accents though," Noah said with a grin.

"I didn't know you guys officially adopted Ernie," J. W. said. "That's great! I hope your process went smoothly like ours with Gabriel."

"Oh yes," Noah said, "his mum signed all rights away the first chance she got, and she's not really sure who the father is. Are you going next, J. W.?"

"Sure I can," J. W. said. "I'm obviously J. W., married to Abby. We have two teenage daughters. One is a brainiac and takes dual enrollment high school and college classes. The other is really smart, also, but enjoys running cross-country and distance track so she just takes AP courses."

"Now, J. W., you're not from around here either, are you?" Mandy asked.

"Oh, is it that obvious?" J. W. laughed. "No, I'm from the U.K. London, actually."

"How did you and Abby meet?" Josh asked.

"She came to London in a study abroad program from the University of Georgia," J. W. explained. "We actually met at a mutual friend's virtual birthday party."

"What do you do?" Mandy said.

"I'm a real estate attorney and developer," J. W. said. "My latest project is an agrihood we're calling Bailey Park Farm out near Holly Springs. We're targeting younger families living in food deserts that want to live close to their food and learn trade skills. We're doing the children's education in learning pods, kind of like the old one-room schoolhouse, through The Virtual Academy in RTP. We've won several awards for community development."

"That's so cool," Mandy said. "I teach seventh-grade math at Kittrell Heights School in Durham. We should talk about those pods sometime . . . and about dyslexia too, Noah. I've got a child who's been passed on that may be right up your alley."

"Right up my what?" Noah said.

"Oh that's just an old Southern slang phrase that means um . . ." Mandy said.

"It's your cup of tea," Abigail said.

"Oh, got it," Noah said.

"I'm from Alabama so you'll have to get used to my idioms," Mandy said with a smile as bright as her blonde hair. "Now J. W., you said something about adopting Gabriel?"

"Yes," J. W. said, "Gabriel is a refugee from Nigeria. Her parents were killed in a genocide war when she was quite young, around one. She came to live with us as a two-year-old. She's got a strong personality and is really bright. We named her Gabriel which means "God is my strength."

Josh said, "What a beautiful name!"

"Yes it is," Mandy said. "Well, I guess it's my turn. I'm Mandy, and Josh and I have been together now for six years, but we're not married so we've chosen not to have any children like Ernie or Gabriel."

"She's chosen," Josh said.

"OK, I've chosen," Mandy answered and then continued. "As I said, I teach seventh-grade math at Kittrell Heights School in Durham, and I'm from Alabama, and that's about it."

Josh leaned forward and said, "I wanted you guys to come over for dinner so Mandy could meet you. She thinks I'm weird because I read the Bible and talk about what I'm learning about Jesus and faith and work. I wanted her to meet some more weird people."

Mandy's smile disappeared slowly. The dining room turned quiet.

Finally, Abigail said, "So, Mandy, how did you and Josh meet?"

Mandy dropped her head and then slowly stood, pushing her chair back carefully. She said, "You'll have to ask him. If you all will please excuse me, I'm suddenly not feeling well. Josh, please serve the pie from the fridge to our guests. Thank you."

With that, she left the dining room and escaped to their bedroom.

The silence was disturbed only by Lemondrop, their yellow Lab, whining by the back door to go out.

Consider How God Nods at You

Read 1 Peter 3:15–16. Recall and share an experience when you or someone you know lacked respect and courtesy in talking about their faith with a pre-believer, i.e., someone who has yet to go "all in" with Jesus. What are your top five guidelines for respect and courtesy in talking about faith?

Discover more about the characters and places you met in this chapter.

Chapter 12

THE FOLLOW-UP

Isla knocked lightly on the door.

"Come in, Isla," said a weak voice from within.

"Hi Daddy," Isla said, trying to use her cheery voice despite the darkness of the room and the struggle in his voice.

"Hello love," Elijah whispered. "How's my brilliant daughter today?"

"I'm well," she said. "What did your doctor say?"

Elijah inhaled deeply and said slowly, "It's not good, dear. The cancer is progressing rapidly now. Stage 4. Soon I'll have to stay home with help. I'm afraid it won't be long."

"Oh Daddy," Isla pleaded. "You must hang on a bit longer. Harper's team is so close to finding the nanoid code. We have the antigen identified. The FDA will green-light the approval process quickly, but you've got to give us some time."

Elijah struggled and said, "My love, I'll do my best, but regardless, you must continue the work so others may live. Discover the treasure within at all costs."

Isla slumped forward in her chair, her head in her hands. She cried softly.

"Promise me you will," Elijah demanded as best he could.

"I promise, Daddy," Isla sobbed. "I promise."

Consider How God Nods at You

Read Psalm 69. Remember and share as best you can a time when you were desperately in search of help and God seemed distant.

Chapter 13
THE PROPOSAL

Join Abigail, Harper, and Josh as they learn more about work as worship in God Nods Resources. Discover more here.

I t's another Wednesday morning at 6:30, which means Abigail, Harper, and Josh are together again in their weekly trio meeting. As Harper said once, "'Trio' is easier to say than 'two or three,' and besides we aren't even close to trinity status."

After discussing the week's Faith Positive Fellowship Resource video, Josh asked to share. "I've been reading in the Bible about marriage," he began, "and I'm thinking that Mandy and I should get married. That my hesitation to marry her is holding back what God wants for us. I'm not sure what's up with Mandy and Jesus, but I know I'm not helping any right now."

"OK," Harper said. "You want us to pray? I'm getting better at that."

"Yes, and how about you two invite her to go with you to the Southern Ideal Home Show this weekend? Say on Saturday?" Josh asked.

"OK, but why?" Abigail asked.

"I'd like to have decorators and caterers come in and transform our home for the evening," Josh said. "I plan to propose."

"That's really sweet, Josh," Abigail said. "I'm sure she'll love it."

"Yea, but what if she says no, and then you're out all that money?" Harper said, poorly stifling a smile.

"Josh, what's been holding you back?" Abigail asked. "Perhaps we can support you in praying about that."

"That would be great," Josh said. "My Father was a wonderful provider and a miserable husband and frankly a miserable father, too. I'm just afraid I'll repeat his mistakes."

"I'm coding up a prayer for you now, buddy," Harper said.

It took some convincing, but the following Saturday morning Mandy joined Abigail and Harper at the Southern Ideal Home Show at Dortna Arena. The three of them strolled along, drooling over the outdoor kitchens. "Josh loves to cook outdoors," Mandy said.

"Noah does, too," Harper said. "I've tried to code him for indoor cooking, but it corrupts every time."

"Speaking of indoor cooking, thanks for coming over last week for dinner. I really enjoyed our time together, at least most of it," Mandy said.

Harper said, "Yea, the food was great, and the company was even better."

"If I may, Mandy," Abigail said, "what turned you away from Jesus when you were younger?"

Mandy stopped and stood perfectly still, staring into Abigail's dark, soulful eyes. Abigail returned her stare, only more softly, with compassion.

"Who told you?" Mandy asked. "Josh doesn't even know so he couldn't tell you. How did you find out?"

"Find out what?" Abigail asked gently.

"You know," Mandy said.

"No, I don't," Abigail responded softly. "I only know I was supposed to ask you that question."

"Well, who told you to ask it?" Mandy said louder, her voice tense and harsh.

"Must have been a God Nod," Harper said.

"A what?" Mandy said, turning on her heels to stare down Harper now, her voice loud enough to draw the attention of others in the outdoor kitchen displays.

"A God Nod," Harper said matter-of-factly. "It's when two or three people get together and Jesus shows up. That's when the fun begins!"

"Well, this question isn't much fun for me," Mandy said and started to cry, softly at first, then louder.

"You want to sit down and talk about it?" Abigail offered.

"Not really, but I suppose it can't hurt any more than it does already," Mandy said. Harper pulled out three chairs at a nearby table. Abigail took some tissues from her purse and handed them to Mandy.

"Well if you must know," Mandy started, "it happened when I joined the youth group at a church in Birmingham. All my friends were going so my folks said I could, too. Besides I'd be in church, and they'd know where I was."

"Had you gone to church much?" Abigail asked.

Mandy answered, "Oh yes, we went a lot when I was younger. But Mama always said after the deacons asked Pastor Bill to resign because he changed the order of worship, she would never go back."

"Sounds right to me," Harper added. "I quit church because . . ."

"Go on Mandy," Abigail interrupted.

"So I hadn't been to church in a long time," Mandy said. "I thought it was safe there. I'll spare you all the details, but let's just say it wasn't safe."

Harper asked, "What do you mean it wasn't safe?"

"Well, this is kind of hard to say," Mandy started, "and I don't want ya'll to think bad of me . . ."

"Mandy, you'll only receive love from us," Abigail promised.

"Well, the youth minister started discipling me . . . in private," Mandy said. "And the next thing I know he's kissing me, and I'm enjoying the attention, and well . . ." Her voice grew quieter and more sullen, as she relived the experience.

"It's OK, Mandy," Abigail said. "That's enough."

"I'm OK," Mandy said. "It took me a lot of counseling just to talk about it like this."

"So, who is this booger? Where do we find him?" Harper asked angrily.

"Harper, that's irrelevant now," Abigail interjected. "Unless Mandy wants to do something about it."

"No, there's nothing to be done," Mandy said. "He told me nobody would believe me anyway. So that's when I stopped going to church and turned away from Jesus. I mean if somebody who works for him acts like that, I want no part of him."

Consider How God Nods at You

Read James 3:1-2 in *The Message*. Share an experience you had when a minister disappointed you or even violated your trust. Please avoid using actual names if your description is public.

"What would it be like for you to forgive him, Mandy? Even though he doesn't deserve it or never asked for it?" Abigail asked.

Mandy smiled through her tears. "Is that another God Nod question?," and all three of them laughed. "Yes, I had to just move on with my life. I had finally forgiven him when Josh and I started dating. And then, after six years together, out of the blue Josh asked me if I knew anything about Jesus. What am I supposed to tell him? I can't say anything to discourage him in his search for Jesus."

"And yet you're still searching for Jesus, too, aren't you?" asked Abigail.

"Yea, and not doing a very good job as you could tell the other night at dinner," Mandy said. "I'm sorry for leaving the table so abruptly. I hope you two can forgive me."

"Already done," Harper said. "I even prayed for you."

"You know, Mandy," Abigail said, "Jesus cares a lot more about who you'll be than who you were."

"That's just it," Mandy replied. "I don't know who I am. I mean, I do, but take my relationship with Josh for instance. He keeps saying we 'might' get married 'some day,' but what does that mean? He's a lot more loving and caring about my feelings since we moved to RTP. He listens a lot better, but he keeps asking me what I think about Jesus, and I don't know what to tell him. I don't know who I am to Jesus."

"What if that's what Josh wants to talk to you about?" Abigail said.

Mandy sat quietly, wiping her tears, which fell faster. "That's definitely a God Nod question!"

Harper joined in. "Try talking with him. Ask him who he thinks Jesus is. Josh is just about all in."

"Really?" Mandy asked. "Well, OK then. I will. I'll talk with him about it tonight."

Abigail and Harper smiled slyly at one another. "Speaking of which, you said you had to be back home in an hour, and you know how Beltline traffic can be even on a Saturday," Harper said.

"OK, you're right. Let me get myself together," Mandy said. "I just want to thank you girls for listening to me, being here for me. I really appreciate it even if I was startled by the God Nods."

"Oh trust me," Harper said. "God Nods startle us, too!"

Consider How God Nods at You

Read Ephesians 2:10. Whom are you in Christ? What work does Jesus have for you to do?

Chapter 14

THE DOWNERS

Isla wiped the tears from her cheeks as best she could and started toward the door.

"Isla," Elijah said. "I love you so much and I'm very proud of you. Your mother would be, too."

She ran back to her daddy and tenderly wrapped his gaunt body in her arms—an embrace into which they both settled, paused, and breathed deeply. The kind of hug exchanged when you're uncertain about what happens next.

Isla turned toward the door, opened it slowly, looked back as her daddy sat down, painfully in his chair, then shut the door lightly. *Now what?* she thought, wiping more tears. *I hate to cry.*

She moved up the hall back toward her office. She looked up and saw Abigail, Harper, and Josh still standing. Isla knocked and opened the door quickly. "Sorry to bother," she said, "but Harper may I see you for a moment when you're done? In my office?"

"Of course," Harper said quickly.

"Thanks," said Isla who then walked toward her office, leaving Abigail's door slightly open.

"I'm about to find out why Isla is on your mind this morning," Harper said to Abigail. "I knew you'd gone and done it, but I didn't think it'd be this quickly."

Abigail said, "Well, I think you're about to find out what an amazing wall-buster Jesus is."

"Yea, OK. Here goes nothing," Harper said and then turned right out of Abigail's door and headed to Isla's office.

"Have you got a minute more, Abby?" Josh asked.

"Sure, have a seat. How may I help?"

"It's Mary Elizabeth," Josh started. "She . . . well, she . . . she's really hard to work with because she's so negative."

"How so?"

"Every time we meet, she's telling me why a new idea won't work. It's been tried before when she worked for another company. It didn't work there and won't work here," Josh said. "And the other day when we had an all-team gathering, I walked up on her talking about how ineffective I am as a leader and how she's amazed we're doing as well as we are."

"That must have stung," Abigail said.

"And pissed me off," Josh said. "I mean that kind of insubordination and poor attitude from someone who last opened a new account twelve months ago is . . . well, grounds for dismissal, right? So, is that enough to get rid of her? Or is there some HR documentation I have to do?"

"May I suggest another approach?" Abigail asked.

"Sure, but it won't work," Josh said.

"Now who sounds like an Eeyore Vampire?" Abigail asked.

"A what?" Josh said.

"You sound like Mary Elizabeth now," Abigail replied. "So let's do this. Go back and reread in *Faith Positive in a Negative World*, chapter 5, about how best to respond like Jesus to those kinds of conversations."

Consider How God Nods at You

Download free and read chapter 5 of *Faith Positive in a Negative World* here.

Josh said, "Oh yeah. I forgot about those three tactics."

"And the two-step," Abigail added. "I'll do a High Performance Pattern assessment with Mary Elizabeth. Ask her to come see me, and I'll explain it to her and coach her through it."

"Oh, that assessment really helped me a great deal," Josh said. "Maybe that's just what she needs."

Discover more about High Performance Patterns and how you and your team can elevate to peak performance.

"And Josh," Abigail said, "when did you last ask Mary Elizabeth how you can best support her?"

"It's been a while," Josh replied. "Last time I did she said there's nothing I can do for her unless I want to help her with household stuff and caring for her two preschoolers. Since her husband left her for their church small-group leader, she's got a lot on her."

"What did you say?" Abigail asked.

"Just said I'm sorry," Josh said. "That's all I had."

"OK, you read and send Mary Elizabeth over to see me," Abigail said. "And I'll pray with you for her . . . and for you. You do pray for her, right?"

Josh dropped his head and stammered, "Not exactly."

Consider How God Nods at You

Read Ephesians 4:11–12. Recall a coworker or someone you lead that is like Mary Elizabeth. Share how you reacted and also how you wish you had responded better.

Please refrain from using anyone's actual name in a public discussion. Instead refer to them as Eeyore Vampires.

Harper timidly knocked on Isla's door. She had her back to it even though it was open. Harper didn't want to intrude so she knocked again, louder.

"Oh hey, Harper," Isla said as she whirled around. "Come on in and have a seat." She took a deep breath and forced a quick smile. "I want to have a meeting with your team."

"OK," Harper said hesitantly, fearful of what would come next. "What would you like to talk about?"

"We don't have much time," Isla said, her voice breaking—then clearing her throat—"to get this pancreatic cancer code figured out."

"Well, we're making great progress," Harper started.

Isla interrupted, "I'm sure you are, but it's not enough. I must speak to your team. When can you get them together?"

"Well, Akorfa is on holiday for about three weeks," Harper said.

"I guess if that's the best you can do . . ." Isla said.

Harper got up to leave, stopped at the door, and turned around and said, "Isla, I've known you and your daddy for a while. You can trust me. Is everything OK?"

"Yes. Sure. Why do you ask?" Isla answered.

"You just seem somewhat . . . um . . . disturbed," Harper said.

Isla straightened up in her desk chair and said quickly, "Everything's fine. Let's do that meeting on Zoom. Send me an invitation, OK?"

"Sure," Harper said and left.

The awkwardness of the conversation clung too tightly for comfort. *I sure could use a God Nod about now*, Harper thought.

Consider How God Nods at You

Read Galatians 6:2. What does it mean to "bear another's burden" at work? How can you "bear another's burden" when they aren't ready to share it yet?

Discover more about the characters
and places you met in this chapter.

Chapter 15
THE SURPRISE

Abigail, Harper, and Josh missed a Wednesday morning Trio gathering or two due to schedule conflicts, which was fine with Harper as long as they met on the Wednesday of Isla's meeting with the coding team. Akorfa was back from holiday so Harper scheduled it for today. And she definitely needed some prayer support for God Nods today!

After discussing the Scripture and video activities from Faith Positive Fellowship Resources for the past few weeks, Abigail said, "Well Josh, how did it go for you on that Saturday night you proposed to Mandy?"

"Yea," Harper chimed in, "what did she say?"

"It was so cool," Josh started. "You know I hired decorators and caterers, right?"

"We remember already," Harper interrupted. "What did she say?"

"OK, OK," Josh smiled that smile. "She said yes!"

Abigail said, "Yeah!"

"Whew," Harper said.

"And she said she'd been waiting for me to ask for three years, ever since we moved in together. Who knew?" Josh said. "I told her she could have asked me, but she said, 'I'm from Alabama, and that's not how we do it.'"

He continued: "So I opened up and told her why it took me three years—about my hesitation because of my Father's miserable relationships and I feared repeating his mistakes. She didn't know that so it took a minute to sink in."

"How did she respond?" Abigail asked.

"She understood, of course, and then apologized for leaving the table abruptly the night you and your husbands were over for dinner. She told me about her experience with the youth minister, which she said she told you two about, right?"

"She did," Harper said. "And?"

"Then we talked about Jesus, who he really is and how much he loves us. I shared with her what I've been reading from Paul about marriage and apologized for holding us—especially her—back from who we're supposed to be—who Jesus wants us to be going forward as a couple and hopefully a family. I didn't care about her past and would pray for Jesus to heal her."

"You said that? About going forward? And not caring about the past?" Abigail asked, hardly able to trust what she heard.

"I did. Was that an OK thing to say?" Josh asked.

Harper said. "It was perfect. And you have no idea how perfect it was. Congratulations friend!"

"And there's one more thing," Josh said. "Mandy and I have something to get your wisdom on. You mind if I Facetime her right now before she leaves for school?"

"That's fine," Abigail said.

Harper said, "Go for it."

Josh got Mandy on the call. "Hey ladies," she said, flashing her engagement ring on the screen.

"CONGRATULATIONS!" Abigail and Harper screamed together.

Mandy said. "Thank you! You should have seen everything Josh had done. It was beautiful."

"OK, Honey, Harper has another meeting in a few minutes so let's tell them what we're thinking and save the rest for later," Josh said. "I've been reading from Paul about baptism, too, and that's a pretty big deal once you're all in with Jesus. So we're both now all in with Jesus, and yet neither of us have been baptized so . . . "

" . . . we were wondering what it would be like," Mandy said, "if we invited the bridal party over here for brunch on our wedding day, and after we eat, Josh and I get baptized in our pool."

"Then everyone can go back home with plenty of time to change clothes for the wedding," Josh said.

"Me included," Mandy said. "And in the beginning of the ceremony, the minister can say that we were baptized together that morning."

"So, what do you think?" Josh asked.

Mandy added, "Yea, what do ya'll say?"

Abigail and Harper stared in disbelief at one another. Then, as if listening to the same voice in their heads, said together, "It's a God Nod!"

Consider How God Nods at You

Read Psalm 139:7–10. Agree or disagree with this statement and support your reasons: God's middle name is "Surprise."

Chapter 16
THE IMPOSSIBLE

Charlotte Wilson continued the TVNZ interview. "Well, Dr. Campbell, I mean Elijah, this body known as Taonga Technologies seemingly does the impossible. How do you do it?"

"What is impossible?" Elijah asked. "We rarely know until we find within the motivation which fuels our imagination that propels us to innovate."

Consider How God Nods at You

Read Matthew 19:26 in *The Message*. How does "every chance if you trust God" transform your view of what is possible and impossible at work?

"What was your initial motivation for Taonga Technologies?" Charlotte asked, leaning in.

Elijah stared off for a moment, inhaled deeply, even slowly, and said, "I told you how important my father was in setting my course. His illness, his contracting a COVID-19 variant, set me on this specific path."

"And that was the first cure you perfected using nanoids, right?" Charlotte said, proud of what she remembered from the press release.

"Yes, but remember we did it as a team," Elijah said, "and unfortunately not in time for my father. I found the antigen too late for him, as Isla did with the nanoid code. Now that I think about it, both of us were driven by grief to our discoveries."

"And that's how new life emerged from certain death?" Charlotte asked.

Elijah's face hinted that faint wisp of a smile again, as if musing on some new truth, and said, "Yes, that's right."

"So your Father's illness was your initial motivation," Charlotte said. "What engaged you to imagine and innovate in such a radical manner?"

"The small victories, Charlotte," Elijah said, his smile larger now. "We knew that the cumulative effect of these small victories would be to win the war, to discover the impossible. So we imagined that we had won, and when you know you have won and the impossible is within grasp, you can try anything, learn from it, and innovate. It's simple, really."

Charlotte laughed this time. "You make it sound simple, Elijah. But for most of us, it's not quite that easy."

"Oh you're right," Elijah chuckled. "Simple and easy are two different matters. And yet the more you do the impossible, the more likely it becomes. We believe the human body was born to heal itself. It just needs some help saving itself, some help doing what it can't do for itself. That's where the nanoids play such a critical role."

"Well, when you say it like that," Charlotte mused, "I almost believe the impossible, too."

Chapter 17

THE CRISIS

"We believe it's a God Nod, too," Mandy exclaimed. "That's what we said, right Josh?"

"Yep, it sure is," Josh said. "Now Honey, Harper has a meeting to go to."

Harper said, "Yea, don't remind me."

Josh stepped away to say goodbye to Mandy and wish her well at Kittrell Heights School that day.

Harper turned to Abigail and said, "I don't want to go to this meeting. You're praying, right?"

"Have been and will continue," Abigail assured her.

Back in her home office, Harper logged into Zoom and opened up the meeting. Isla popped up for admission immediately. Harper let her in.

Isla said, "You do remember I'm leading this meeting, right?"

"Of course and good morning, Isla," Harper said.

"Good morning," Isla muttered.

Harper admitted Carl, Akorfa, and the rest of the team, and Isla began quickly, her voice caustic and strained. "It's urgent that we move forward more quickly with the nanoid coding for the pancreatic cancer antigen. People die daily from this dreaded disease, and we have to stop it. The FDA has green-lighted us for the fast track to approval, but you know that's a slow, ponderous process at best. We have to get to market ASAP. Now where are you?"

Silence was the only response, almost as if the team all took a step back. Harper opened her mouth to speak, but Isla cut her off. "Carl, where are you on this?"

"We're enjoying some small victories, Isla," Carl said. "We have had some significant breakthroughs. We think we've found the code for the white blood cell antigen production, but the self-destruction sequence is proving trickier this time around. Akorfa . . ."

Isla interrupted, "That's not good enough, Carl. The nanoids should already be programmed for self-destruction. You have the previous sequence to work from. What's your problem?"

Carl stammered, and opened his mouth wider as if the words were stuck in his throat. "I . . . I . . . can't . . ." and with that he fell face forward onto his desk.

"Carl!" Isla screamed. "What's your problem?"

Harper realized Carl was in distress, picked up her phone and called 911. Finishing her call, she said, "Carl, if you can hear me, EMS is on the way."

"Will somebody tell me what's going on?" Isla screamed.

Harper said calmly, "Isla, Carl has had a heart attack or stroke or something. EMS is on the way. And I'm going to let his wife, Sally, know now." And with that Harper ended the meeting.

Harper texted Mandy. Sally worked at Kittrell Heights School with Mandy but in the English Department. Harper asked Mandy to let Sally know immediately about Carl's condition.

Fifteen minutes later Mandy texted Harper: "Carl going to Pax Hospital. Not good."

Harper texted Abigail and Josh, both of whom were in their home offices, to tell them about Carl's situation and Isla's reaction. They jumped on a Zoom call together quickly to pray for Carl and Sally . . . and Isla.

"Jesus, you promised to be with us when two or more of us gathered," Abigail began. When she finished praying, the three of them agreed to clear their calendars and go to Pax Hospital to support Carl and Sally.

Meanwhile Isla sat, head in her hands, at her desk, staring down, muttering, "Daddy, what can I do to help you now?"

Consider How God Nods at You

Read Proverbs 16:9. Share a work experience when you expected one outcome and something far different happened. What was your reaction? Your later response?

Chapter 18
THE BENDING

Isla sat staring at her screen, paralyzed by the reality that her only hope, the one chance she had of saving her daddy, had slipped away. She had done everything she knew to do. She was out of options. Her daddy was about to die, and she was powerless to save him.

Her phone buzzed. It was her daddy.

She wiped her face again. She knew her red eyes would give away how upset she was.

"Hi Daddy," she said, cutting off her camera.

"Isla," Elijah said. "Why is your camera off? Please turn it on. I want to see you."

"Oh, sorry, Daddy," Isla said.

"Are you all right? I heard about Carl and the meeting," Elijah asked.

Isla inhaled slowly. Bad news travels quickly. "And what did you hear?" she asked.

"That he had a cardiac event or something during the call," Elijah said, "as he tried to answer your questions about where we are on the nanoid coding for the pancreatic cancer cure."

"OK, that's right," Isla said.

Elijah continued, "How hard were you pushing him, Isla?"

"Pretty hard, I suppose," she said. "You know how intense I can be."

The conversation struggled to breathe for a moment, as if all the air had left the call.

Isla found her words. "Daddy, I don't want to lose you the way we did your father," she said. "I don't want to be too late to save you. This is pancreatic cancer we're talking about."

"I understand," Elijah said. "And I appreciate your concern. But what about Carl and his family? Where is your concern for them?"

Isla looked up, startled that her daddy would express such concern for them knowing his own diagnosis. Something within her shifted, a painful tearing away of perspective from the darkness to open up to more light. "What should I do?" she asked.

"Find out which hospital he's in and go there to check on him," Elijah answered. "I can't go. The risk is too great. Go for us. We'll talk more later about me."

Consider How God Nods at You

Read Ephesians 3:20 in *The Message*. What needs bending within your ego to move you toward greater awareness of and action toward the "Spirit deeply and gently within" you?

Chapter 19
THE VISIT

Harper walked through the Pax Healthcare bioscanner thinking about what happened in the four seconds it took her to pass through it. After all, product development was her specialty. The chip reader downloaded her vital stats including medical history of nanoid transfusions, all stored on a pin-dot behind her ear. "Amazing," she said out loud.

Approved, she took the elevator to the third floor where Sally sat alone, balled up in a chair, arms wrapped tightly around herself. Harper moved near her and said, "Sally?"

"Oh Harper, it's you," she said, unfolded quickly and stood. "Carl is returning from testing any moment. His room is this way," and she led Harper down the hall to discover that Carl was already back.

"Guess I messed up that meeting," Carl said to Harper with a pained look.

Harper said, "It's OK, but next time can you be a little less dramatic?"

They both laughed. Sally looked first at Carl, then Harper, and decided it was an inside joke.

"So, what did they say, dear?" Sally asked.

Carl replied, "I have five artery blockages, and as soon as an OR opens, I'm going in for surgery. They expect no problems bypassing them, but I do have some minimal heart damage."

"They expect no problems, but . . ." Harper said, as she read Carl's face.

"But one of them is the main artery, the widow-maker they call it, and it could be a problem," Carl answered. "How did you know there was something else?"

Harper smiled and said, "We'll talk more later."

A light knock came on the door and in walked Abigail and Josh. "May we come in?"

"Of course," Carl said, "you can save me from Harper!" and everyone laughed.

Harper's phone buzzed and she excused herself. Abigail and Josh stepped up to the bedside to get apprised of Carl's situation. Harper returned and said, "That was Isla. She wanted to know which hospital you're at. She's coming to see you."

Carl's face blanched. Sally took his hand and squeezed it. "It'll be OK, Honey."

Harper looked at Abigail who nodded back at her. A nurse walked in and said, "Sir, the OR attendants are on their way to get you and take you back."

Carl said, "OK, thanks . . . I think."

Abigail stared at Harper who mouthed "OK" and turned to Carl. "Carl, Sally, would it be OK if we prayed together before this surgery?"

Carl stammered, "It's been so long, I'd hardly know what to say."

"Oh, I can pray out loud for us if that's good with you," Harper heard herself offer.

Sally answered this time, "That's just fine with us." She squeezed Carl's hand and reached for Harper's who said, "Oh! OK!" and then turned for Abigail's hand who found Josh's. Their heads bowed together, Harper began their prayer.

"Jesus, it's me, Harper again. Only this time I've got Carl and Sally, Abby and Josh with me. You promised when two or more of us get together, you're with us. So here we are, Jesus, and we really need you here right now."

Unknown to those praying, Isla stepped into the room through the slightly opened door. She stood, unsure of what to do or say. She heard Harper talking . . . to Jesus.

It had been years since Isla heard anyone talk to Jesus. She remembered Mother talking to him and wondering who he was. She heard Mother from the sunroom some mornings, talking to Jesus as if he sat beside her on the wicker sofa. She paused as if Jesus talked, too. Only Isla never could hear him the way Mother did.

She then remembered that the day Mother died, they were supposed to go get ice cream and talk about this Jesus. "It's time you meet him for yourself," she said.

Following her death, when Isla tried to ask Daddy if he knew Mother's Jesus and what he could tell her about him, his only response was, "I don't know him." When Daddy sent her to Chatham Hall, Isla stopped asking about Jesus.

And now here he was again, this Jesus. She assumed Mother's and Harper's Jesus was the same guy. "How could Harper know Jesus, too?" she wondered. So she stepped closer to the circle and listened.

Harper continued to pray, asking Jesus to take good care of Carl, to place his hand on the surgeon's hands to guide the scalpel and every other person and piece of equipment used. "We know Carl belongs to you," Harper prayed, "and that nothing, not even heart surgery, can separate him from your love."

Isla looked up abruptly. *Carl? Belongs to Jesus, too?* she thought.

Harper continued her sincere prayer, thanking Jesus for being present with them now, even as he was present in the T2 meeting earlier. "And Jesus, please be present with Isla as she drives here and keep her close in your presence as well. Grant her the wisdom needed to lead all of us to discover the treasures within, especially the coding for curing pancreatic cancer."

Isla staggered backwards and found a chair. *Mother prayed numerous mornings for Jesus to be present with me. The same words Harper used. And Harper . . . Harper prayed to Jesus for me after the way I treated her and Carl and the rest of the team. How can this be?*, Isla thought.

Harper's "Amen" was followed by Abigail's "Oh Isla! We didn't hear you come in. Were you waiting long?"

"Long enough," Isla said, unable to move from the chair.

"Carl, the OR attendants are here to take you to surgery," the nurse announced.

"Thank you, Harper," Carl said looking into Harper's eyes, finding her soul, and giving it a squeeze. "I am at peace regardless of what happens because I know Jesus is with me. That was a beautiful prayer."

"Yes, it was," Sally said. "Now kiss me old man," and with that Sally kissed Carl, a loud smack that prompted chuckles throughout the room. Except Isla. She still couldn't move.

"Uh ma'am," the attendant said to Isla, "that chair needs to be moved so we can maneuver the bed through the door."

"Oh, of course," Isla stuttered, and somehow stood and moved the chair into the corner.

Consider How God Nods at You

Read Romans 8:38-39. In your work experience, what seemed at one time to be able to separate you from Christ? What about your personal experience? How did Christ stay connected with you in both of these situations?

Chapter 20
THE QUESTIONS

The OR attendants wheeled Carl through the door and turned right down the hall. The nurse announced, "He returns here after his recovery so if you wish to remain, that's great. There is a more open seating area down the hall to your left. It's an atrium."

"Thank you," Sally said.

Now able to move, Isla went quickly to Harper. "Will you please join me in the atrium? I have some questions," she said.

"Sure," Harper said, turned around and whispered to Abigail, "Pray for me."

Abigail whispered back, "God Nod."

Harper smiled and followed Isla down the hall.

Consider How God Nods at You

Read Isaiah 41:10. If you were Harper, what thoughts would you have right now as you walk down the hall to the atrium with Isla?

Chapter 21
THE WAY

Elijah shook his head as he hung up the phone. *Isla is brilliant in so many ways,* he thought to himself, *and yet people are such a challenge for her. I wish her mother were here to help. She'd know what to do.*

He spun his chair around to face the back wall. There hung, written in calligraphy, were his father's final words. He could still see his dad's smiling face, all aglow as if lit from his very soul, as he said these words with one of his final breaths.

"Ah! Discover the treasure . . . of God's presence . . . within."

Elijah thought, *I only wish he had explained himself.*

Consider How God Nods at You

Read Galatians 2:20. What does it mean for you to be created in the image and likeness of God and for Christ to live in you? How does this knowledge affect your work style?

Chapter 22
THE TRUTH

The atrium was empty except for the succulent plants, stunning water features, and streaming sunlight. Harper was relieved and peaceful, which was different for her going into a one-to-one with Isla.

"What were you doing when I entered Carl's room?" Isla asked.

Somewhat taken back, Harper smiled and said, "I was praying."

"Where did you get that prayer?" Isla wondered.

"What do you mean?" Harper said.

"From a book online? Who wrote that prayer?" Isla asked.

"Oh," Harper replied, "I found it in my head. Maybe a little from my heart, too."

Isla couldn't believe what she heard. "Why did you pray for me?"

"I pray for you daily, Isla," Harper said. "I'm a leader myself and understand the responsibilities and pressures, although not on as grand a scale as you. So I pray for you daily. Is that OK?"

Isla sat quietly, head down, listening to the nearby water feature trickle into the koi pond. Suddenly sunshine bathed the floor in front of her. She looked up after it, through the skylights to see a cloud parting, revealing the sun. She smiled.

"Yes, it's OK if you pray for me, Harper," Isla said. "I just didn't know you pray. And so well."

"Hey, you should hear Abby pray," Harper replied. "Prayer is one of her superpowers. I'm a novice."

"I haven't heard anyone pray for me in a long time," Isla responded, lost in her own reverie. "My mother sat in our sunroom each morning and prayed. I remember hearing her say what you said, asking Jesus to be present with me. I don't even know what that means. We were going out for ice cream so she could introduce me to Jesus the day she . . . died. Every time I asked Daddy who Jesus is, he claimed not to know him."

Josh walked up and asked, "May I get you two some coffee? Or water?"

"A bottle of water would be great," Harper said.

Isla added, "Yea, me too" and returned to her thoughts.

"I'll be right back," Josh said.

Harper sat quietly, unsure of what to say. Abigail helped her learn recently in a Faith Positive Fellowship discussion that when Psalm 46:10 says, "Be still" (KJV) that it also means be quiet until God gives you something to say. So she sat quietly, with all of the restraint she had.

Josh returned with their water. Isla reached for her purse and Josh said, "No worries."

Isla looked up at him and then at Harper who smiled. "Josh, you've recently discovered who Jesus is. What can you tell Isla?" she said.

Josh's eyes widened, followed by his signature smile. "Sure," he said, sitting down in a nearby chair. "It all began when I saw the job posting for T2's business development position. As I read it, I felt pulled in."

"What do you mean?" Isla asked.

Josh explained, "I didn't know at first. I knew I could do the job, no sweat. But it was the company's mission that captured my imagination. 'Discover the treasure within.' After I read it, I couldn't get it off my mind."

"What's this got to do with Jesus?" Isla said.

"Good question!" Josh replied. "I searched online for what to call this pull. Shawn Achor's book *The Happiness Advantage* kept appearing. It's an older one, but there's a section that talks about how your work can be a job, a career, or a calling. Calling is when your work is significantly aligned with who you are. So I started searching for 'calling' online, and that's when the book, *Jesus Calling* showed up. I had heard about Jesus one time so I decided to see what he had to do with calling."

"What did you find?" Isla asked, captured by Josh's story.

"First, I got the *Jesus Calling* book and read it," Josh said. "It turns out Jesus is God who came to earth, went back to heaven, and yet still is present here. I don't understand all about how Jesus works, but I'm learning more."

"So that's why Mother asked Jesus to be present with me," Isla said. "Because God is still here. And you, Harper," she said now looking up at Harper, "prayed the same thing."

"It's so easy to feel alone, Isla," Harper said. "Isolated. Carrying the weight of the world by yourself. Especially with all of the pressures and adversity of work and life today."

"Yea, I know," Isla said. "I've never felt as alone as when Mother died. And now Daddy is dying."

Harper and Josh looked at each other in disbelief.

"Did you just say 'Daddy is dying'?" Josh asked.

"Yes, he is in stage 4 with . . . pancreatic cancer," she said, choking on the words.

Harper's head dropped. "And that's why you're pushing us so hard to finish the coding," she said.

Isla's tears fell gently from her cheek onto the water bottle in her hand, their rhythm syncopating with the water feature's trickle. She sobbed lightly. "He doesn't have long to live," she said. "And if I don't save him, I'll be all alone forever."

Harper and Josh sat stunned. They were clueless previously. And yet now that they knew, so much about Isla made sense. The sun peeked out from behind a cloud, immersing the three in partial light.

Finally, Harper spoke. "Isla, there's someone I must call. Please excuse me," and she got up and left. Josh looked after her, resisted the urge to run, and then for some reason he didn't understand said, "Isla, may I tell you more about Jesus?"

Isla looked up and, through red-swollen eyes that were more desperate than Josh had ever seen in anyone, said, "Please."

Consider How God Nods at You

Imagine you are Josh. What would you tell Isla about Jesus? And how?

Join Abigail, Harper, and Josh in the
online God Nods Resource,
Be Still and Know.

Chapter 23
THE LIFE

Harper found a corner of the atrium, away from Isla and Josh, where the sun's rays bathed a ten-foot-tall succulent. A nearby water feature splashed joyfully as if spraying a fountain of water six feet high was its created purpose. The comfy, overstuffed chair beckoned Harper to sit. So she did.

"Akorfa," Harper said, "thanks for answering. I know it's 3:00 AM in Ghana, but I really need to talk with you. Can you wake up?"

Akorfa laughed gently. Harper heard a baby cooing in the background. "It's fine, Harper," Akorfa said. "I'm feeding Nathan."

"Oh," Harper said. "Oh. Sorry to interrupt. Can you talk work and feed?"

"Of course," Akorfa said, "I'm delighted to help you. How may I serve you, my fearless leader?"

Now Harper laughed gently. "I'll catch you up soon on the latest God Nods. You won't believe what's going on," she said.

"What about Carl? How is he?" Akorfa asked.

Harper replied, "He's in surgery. They're bypassing five blockages. We pray he will recover fully."

"And Henry? How is he?" Akorfa asked, remembering Carl's grandson's dire condition.

"Much better now," Harper answered. "The chemo worked and the stem cells are rapidly growing. Now let me ask you something. You came to me recently and asked to experiment with some coding outside of our normal protocols."

"Oh yes, of course," Akorfa replied. "You told me I'd either lost my mind or I would find it" and laughed so loudly baby Nathan squeaked.

"Yea, that's the time," Harper chuckled. "So, what ever became of your efforts?"

"The most incredible thing happened," Akorfa said. "I had a dream about how to code the self-destruct sequence. Well, it really wasn't about that. It was about a traffic jam and how I got out of it when everyone else was stuck at the intersection."

"Really?" Harper said. "How did that work out for you?"

Akorfa said, "I'll tell you more later when Nathan isn't latched on." Harper heard more squeaks and grunts.

"Oh sure. Sorry," Harper said. "Fast-forward to the results, please."

"Well, that's what Carl and I were about to tell Isla in our meeting," Akorfa said. "We have tested the new code rigorously and gotten excellent results. But we need her to sign off on an additional budget expenditure for one more testing round that wasn't initially planned."

Harper sat still. The sun's warmth cascaded down her neck, and the waterfall caressed her ears. Time stood still. Harper inhaled deeply of the richness of converging resources and exhaled a once obscure, now obvious decision.

Consider How God Nods at You

Read 2 Corinthians 9:8-11 in *The Message*. How would you pray if you believed God's timing and resources were available at work?

"Do it," Harper said. "I'll inform Isla. You'll get the credit when it's successful and if she kicks it back, I'll take the blame. Just go do it. Start today. Please."

Nathan gurgled. Akorfa chuckled lightly and said, "You got it, friend."

"And let me know as soon as you know the results, please," Harper said. Akorfa agreed as Nathan nodded off.

Harper smiled. Sometimes, she decided, God Nods are treasures within.

Consider How God Nods at You

Read James 1:5 in *The Message*. How do you make difficult decisions? What did Harper do that you could adopt or adapt?

Discover more about the characters
and places you met in this chapter.

Chapter 24
THE FORGIVENESS

"I'll need to ask Abby and Harper, but I'm sure they'll welcome you, too," Josh said to Isla as Harper walked up.

"Of course we will," Harper said, "but what are we welcoming you to?"

Josh replied, "Isla wants to join us on Wednesday mornings at 6:30 for our Faith Positive Fellowship and learn more about Jesus and what it means to be all in at work."

"That'd be awesome!" Harper said. "I know Abby will be just as delighted as we are."

"Delighted about what?" Abigail said as she walked up on the trio.

"I'd like to join you on Wednesday mornings and learn more about Jesus," Isla said, her voice hopeful. Abigail smiled big, joining Harper and Josh.

She said, "I would be more than delighted, Isla. I'm ecstatic! And I have good news about Carl. He's out of surgery and it was successful. They expect an almost complete recovery."

As Isla rode home, her mind stopped racing, the stress knots in her stomach untied, and somehow she recalled and hummed a song Mother used to sing. She hadn't thought of it in years. What was the name of it?

Seems like the first line is something about fighting voices in my head, Isla remembered. *And it talks about never measuring up*, she went on, *and not belonging.*

"Oh wait! I remember now," Isla said out loud. "Car, play 'You Say' by Lauren Daigle."

"Anything for you, Isla. We'll get home before the song finishes. Do you wish to sit and listen until it's completed?"

"Yes, please," Isla replied. As much as she despised crying, she did it again as the song started, its simple piano opening transported her back to more carefree days when she and Mother shared their love of literature.

"I'm grateful not to be driving," she thought as the auto-car turned right and headed down her street. "I wouldn't be able to see."

Consider How God Nods at You

Play Lauren Daigle's "You Say". Share an experience when a song touched you deeply, calling back memories of previous days. What lyrics especially stand out in your memory? Why are they significant? Include a link to the song so others may enjoy it.

A week later Isla found herself in Abigail's office on Wednesday morning at 6:30, wondering where to sit. She thought, "There are four chairs, and yet . . ."

"Good morning, Isla!" Josh said, "sit anywhere. I'll get an extra chair from my office."

"But there are already four chairs," Isla said. "Why do you need a fifth?"

Josh smiled and said, "Jesus could sit on the floor, but he prefers a chair."

Isla's puzzled face greeted Abigail as she walked in. Josh said, "Tell Isla why we need a fifth chair, Abby."

"Oh yeah, well, it's our way of inviting Jesus to join us," Abigail said. "He told us when two or more of us gather, he's with us. We like the literal manifestation of his presence so we keep a chair open for him."

The Faith Positive Fellowship video for the week focused on forgiveness and creating a forgiveness culture at work. Rather than avoiding mistakes at all costs, innovation grows best in the soil of making new mistakes faster, learning from them, and moving forward quickly to integrate the new learning. A forgiveness culture is the bedrock of innovation.

"On a scale of one to ten," Abigail asked, "how would you rate T2's forgiveness culture? With one being the lowest and ten being the highest?"

The silence clung like a wet, wool blanket to each of them. Finally, Isla spoke. "Based on the last meeting I had with the coding team, I'd say about a two."

More silence and then Abigail asked, "How can we improve the forgiveness factor in our culture so we innovate better?"

Again Isla spoke. "I need to ask forgiveness from your team, Harper. When can we do that?"

"When would you like to?" Harper asked.

Isla replied, "Sooner rather than later."

"We meet at 1:00 PM today," Harper replied.

"I'll be there if you'll send me a Zoom invitation," Isla promised.

Consider How God Nods at You

Read Matthew 18:21–22. How would you rate your company's forgiveness culture on a scale of one to ten? What can you do personally to improve it?

The coding team meeting started early with Akorfa showing off baby Nathan who cooed and smiled on command at the camera as if he had Zoomed his whole life. "He just ate so he's happy," Akorfa explained.

"So cute," Harper said. "We're privileged to have Carl back with us today. Carl, how are you feeling?"

"Well, unlike Nathan, I have yet to eat so I feel like a truck ran over me, but other than that I'm great," Carl laughed.

Harper said, "Hang in there, buddy. I'm sure Sally wants you around, as does Henry. How is he, by the way?"

"Improving daily," Carl said. "The stem cells continue to grow rapidly. But he can't understand why I can't pick him up yet. I keep showing him where they cracked my chest open, but he doesn't get it. Just says, 'Pops have boo-boo?'"

Harper said, "Pops has a big boo-boo. Glad to hear he's progressing nicely. OK team, we're also privileged to have Isla back with us today. Isla, thanks so much for joining us. We know you're busy and your time is valuable."

"As is your team's, Harper," Isla began. "Let me get right to the point. I'd like to apologize today and ask your forgiveness for my behavior last time we were together. I have no excuse other than I forgot who we are and how we best treat one another. I hope you can forgive me," and she dropped her head in penitence.

While no one was muted, the silence was palatable. Then slowly at first, to a person, each team member said, "Of course we do" or "Most assuredly" or "It's all good."

Isla's head raised a little more with each expression of forgiveness. "I don't deserve your forgiveness, and yet I thank you for it."

Harper said, "We all need forgiveness. We're all broken in some way."

Akorfa added, "That's why we do what we do as T2. We're broken and need help to 'discover the treasure within.'"

"Thank you so much for the reminder, Akorfa," Isla said. "Harper, there's something else if I may."

Harper said, "Of course. Please go ahead."

"I want to share something confidentially with you that may help you understand some of my recent behavior," Isla began. "I'm not asking you to excuse it. Just understand it better."

She inhaled deeply, wondering to herself if she could do this. *Transparency isn't my strength*, she thought.

She moved forward. "I'm going to trust you with this which is difficult for me. And yet it's necessary."

She took another breath, exhaled an inaudible "Help me, please Jesus" and said, "My daddy, our founder, Dr. Elijah

Campbell, has stage 4 pancreatic cancer."

The gasps were audible as the coding team, scattered all over the planet, corporately experienced the shock and hurt such news brings.

"We've known for a while," Isla continued, "only now he's no longer responding to treatments. And of course the cancer is progressing faster."

Akorfa responded first. "Oh Isla," she said. "I am so sorry."

"Yea, me too," Carl said. "I kind of understand where you are from Henry's experience. And I now understand why you pushed us so urgently."

It was Harper's turn. "Isla, how may we best help?"

"The answer is simple yet profound, obvious yet elusive: finish the coding sequence before Daddy runs out of time," Isla said and immediately started crying softly. She reached quickly to mute herself and turn off her camera.

"Team," Harper said, "the task before us now has an importance like none other. By whatever means necessary, we must save Elijah's life. We have to discover this treasure within. The taonga is within our reach. Let's go get it. Akorfa, how may we best support you?"

Consider How God Nods at You

Read Matthew 6:34. How do you imagine the impossible can be done in your work? What role do your focus and your faith in God combine to catalyze your efforts?

Chapter 25
THE PRESCRIPTION

"And yet, I'm sure TVNZ viewers want to know," Charlotte continued, "how do you actually do the impossible?"

"We have a prescription for that, Charlotte," Elijah responded quickly, as if he expected this question. "It's attention plus intention plus action equals positive results."

"OK, let's break that down," Charlotte said. "What do you mean by *attention*?"

"Attention is the scarcest of human resources," Elijah replied. "You focus your thoughts and relationships and give the most important and positive ones your attention."

"Attention goes to thoughts and relationships," Charlotte said, "that are important and positive. What about *intention*?"

"Your emotions shape your intentions, your stated desires for what you wish to do—your imagined outcomes including those that seem impossible at the moment," Elijah said. "Our

Taonga Technologies mission is to discover the treasure within," he continued, "which states clearly our intention as a company and captures the imagination of all of us who work there."

"Which first captured your imagination and therefore shaped your intention as a child when your father spoke those words to you," Charlotte said, connecting the dots for her viewers and herself.

"Yes, that's it. And yet attention and intention lack one key ingredient in the prescription," Elijah said, "which is *action*. Until someone acts, the impossible remains impossible. When you act, do something to express your new learnings, what some regard as miracles happen."

"And that's how you discovered the body has white blood cell antigens that can heal," Charlotte said. "You gave attention to the antigens, intended to discover them, and acted until you did."

"That's it, Charlotte. Exactly!" Elijah said, excited she caught on so quickly.

"And it all begins with attention to thoughts and relationships," Charlotte mused. "Where is your attention right now, Elijah?"

Consider How God Nods at You

Which of these three prescription ingredients—attention, intention, action—is most challenging for you at work? What are some ways you can overcome these challenges? Pick one of these ways. When will you start doing it?

Chapter 26
THE ATTENTION

"Thank you so much for asking, Harper," Akorfa said. "Since taking the lead on working with our team on finalizing the pancreatic cancer self-destruct sequence, my greatest challenge has been focusing my attention on this monumental task."

"You've had lots of additional work to do since my bypass surgery," Carl said. "Sorry about that."

"Carl," Harper said, "where are you on getting back up to speed?"

"I'm close," Carl said. "I hope within a week."

"And as you know Nathan requires lots of my time and energy," Akorfa said, holding up the now sleeping baby.

"I can't even imagine," Isla said.

"What I'd like to ask you for, Isla and Harper," said Akorfa, "is approval to work exclusively for the next two weeks on final testing of the code for the self-destruct sequence within the pancreatic cancer nanoid. I believe that with this kind of focused attention, I can complete the necessary testing. Also, as I need assistance, I'd like for my requests to take team members' priority over other projects."

Akorfa's request settled on the team, cast against the urgent backdrop of Elijah's dire situation. As it settled, almost simultaneously they began to nod in agreement, speaking words of support for Akorfa, pledging to do whatever it took to ensure the sequence was coded quickly.

"Isla," Harper said, "it sounds as if the team wishes to honor Akorfa's request."

"Indeed it does," Isla said, "and may I thank each of you for focusing your attention on this matter. It's certainly urgent to me as he is the only parent I have remaining," and with that her voice broke, and she cast her eyes away from the camera, then cut off her video.

Harper said, "Isla, we are of one mind on this matter. Akorfa, thank you. Team, thank you! Let's get this done for Elijah."

Consider How God Nods at You

Read James 1:6-16. James encourages us to pray boldly, believing. What are some projects at work that could use your bold, believing prayers?

Chapter 27
THE LIES

A bigail stared at the sun-touched philodendron on her desk, her mind lost in thought and prayer.

"Father, you know Elijah's situation," she said. "You know we are so close to finding the cure. What's holding us back?"

She suddenly became aware of the sun rising through her window, it's golden-orange rays spilling into her home office and brightening everything in its path.

"There is a spiritual answer to this problem," she decided. And with that she opened the latest month's Faith Positive Fellowship resource, hoping for an answer.

"You really do see what you look for," she said with a smile.

The new month's course title was "The 5 Lies that Stop Your Action."

"This is exactly what we need," she said as she messaged Harper, Josh, and Isla. "Let's do this immediately."

Consider How God Nods at You

Do you agree or disagree with Abigail when she said, "There is a spiritual answer to this problem," i.e., the lack of a break-through in coding the pancreatic cancer sequence? Explain why. Share an experience when you and/or your team found a spiritual answer to a similar "stuck" problem.

The quartet decided to commit one hour per day for a week unpacking the 5 Lies, one lie per day starting the following Monday, in a focused-attention cadence to discover how to beat the clock winding down in Elijah's pancreatic cancer war. "We can win the fight within," Abigail said to the team, "as we work for a miracle."

Consider How God Nods at You

Read 1 John 4:4. Name one action you can take in your company to work for a miracle because Christ in you is greater than the liar in the world.

Abigail opened their gathering the following Monday. "The video explains that intention is an expression of the Believe core practice, or our emotional engagement with our work," she said, "and yet divorced from attention and action, intention is the road to nowhere."

"Which is where we are right now," Isla said, "close but nowhere."

"But we have Akorfa who is now giving uber attention to the coding sequence. And the team agreed to respond immediately to her requests for help," Harper said.

"So you're acting quickly," Josh added.

"The attention plus intention plus action prescription is in play," Abigail added.

Isla quickly asked, "Then why do we still lack a breakthrough?"

"Well let's look at the first of the 5 Lies," Abigail said. "The first lie is, if you wonder if you belong to God, then you don't, based on Luke 4:1–11. What's this about?"

"Satan's temptation of Jesus," Josh said. "Satan wants Jesus to exchange his relationship with God for one with him. That's why he keeps saying, 'If you're the Son of God, . . .'"

"Which questions his identity, who he is," Harper said.

Each of them stared off in a different direction, contemplating their own identity in Christ.

"Identity has been a big sticking point for me," Isla slowly confessed. "Understanding that Christ is in me, that I am created in the image and likeness of God, and the difference it makes is tough for me to believe some days."

"Yea, me, too," Harper continued. "That's why I quit going to church and praying and even my relationship with God. If what I knew to be true from my experience with *Jesus Calling* was false, then I had nothing left in my relationship. So I walked away from all of it."

"You did, but," Abigail interjected, "when you came to me about a personnel situation, you asked me to pray. So you knew at some level that God still has relationships with us."

Harper paused and answered, "I did. However, I didn't think Jesus wanted one with me. Sarah Young writes about Jesus's presence with me personally—she writes in first person like she's talking for Jesus—and if that was false, well, none of the rest mattered."

"And yet you now see that as a lie," Josh asked. "What moved you back to Jesus?"

"Honestly, it was Abby," Harper said quickly. "Well, it was Christ in her. She assured me that Jesus loved me regardless of what that minister said. And then she loved on me like Jesus would, in a whole 1 Corinthians 13 kind of way."

Consider How God Nods at You

Read 1 Corinthians 13. What does Harper mean by "a whole 1 Corinthians 13 kind of way"? How do you work from these definitions of love?

"And that's what you did with me, Harper," Isla said with a smile. "Even when I was at my worst, a hot mess in that team meeting. Even when I came to the hospital to see Carl and took you away from Sally for a couple of hours, you just loved me and showed me Jesus. I can never repay you for that."

Harper dabbed at her right eye with her sleeve.

"Harper," Abigail said, "are you crying?"

"Shut up, friend," Harper replied with a smile. "Isla, I was just passing it on."

Josh spoke up. "So our identity is in Christ because of the image and likeness God put in us that's redeemed by him. So the lie is a lie because the Bible tells us nothing can separate us from

God's love in Jesus. And we show one another that as we love God and others more."

"Pretty much," Harper said.

Isla said, "Sounds right to me."

"And remember that Jesus used the truth of Scripture to combat the lie of a broken relationship with God," Abigail added. "So giving attention to Scripture daily decimates this lie."

"I can see," Isla said, "how doubting you're in relationship with God can inhibit a breakthrough. It lessens your God confidence, which keeps you from acting boldly."

Harper added, "Akorfa acted boldly asking for two weeks to work only on this project. She's giving attention to her intention and acting on it. See what I did there?"

The quartet laughed.

Consider How God Nods at You

Read Luke 4:1–11. Describe how you understand your identity in Christ as it relates to your work.

Tuesday morning found the quartet together again, always at 6:30.

Josh began this time. "The second lie," he said, "is if it seems like God plays favorites, it's because he does, based on James 2:1–13."

Isla replied, "This lie challenges me especially. We can't seem to find the breakthrough so it seems like God does play favorites, and we're not one."

"I know what you mean," Harper added. "I think of myself as the person wearing rags who gets shown to the back-row seat. And yet even as Abby said to me that God loved even me, I felt this oppressive lie lifting."

"I'm sure I didn't say, 'Even you,' Harper," Abigail said quickly.

"Well," Harper said, "that's what it seemed like. And yet this passage clears up this notion of God plays favorites. I like verse 5: 'Isn't it clear by now that God operates quite differently? He chose the world's down-and-out as the kingdom's first citizens, with full rights and privileges.' Sounds like if God does play favorites, it's on the side of the underdogs."

Josh said, "Yes, but it goes on to say: 'This kingdom is promised to anyone who loves God.' Anyone, regardless of how much your suit did or didn't cost. Or how successful you are in achieving breakthroughs."

"So the fact we haven't cracked the code," Isla said slowly, "doesn't mean we're not God's favorites."

"It just means," Abigail said, "that we have yet to crack it. And the kingdom of God where miracles happen is still ours because we love him."

"And since God loves underdogs and I'm from Down Under, we're really close to that breakthrough," Harper said with a laugh. The quartet joined her laughter, each of them joining Isla as she settled into this new reality.

As the laughter drifted away, Josh's yellow Lab, Lemondrop, who came to work that day, pawed at the office door, wanting to get in.

Consider How God Nods at You

Read James 2:1-13. What do you believe? Does God play favorites? How do your responses to others based on their under-dog appearance reflect God's responses to "anyone"?

Harper opened the quartet's Wednesday morning meeting with, "The third lie is if you wish others well, that relieves you from helping them. James 2:14–17 is the primary Scripture passage. If ever there was a case of 'Intention is the road to nowhere when it's divorced from action,' this is it."

Isla said, "I learned this truth personally when I did such a poor job of leading your team meeting, Harper, when Carl had his heart attack."

"What do you mean, Isla?" Josh asked.

"My intention was to motivate the team to do more and faster," Isla replied. "What I actually did was the opposite because I acted differently from my intention. The lie is my talk was enough, but no one could hear what I was saying for how I said it. All talk. No walk."

"Oh, now I understand," Josh said. "I've been guilty of that with Mary Elizabeth. Abigail helped me find actions that aligned with my intention better and held me accountable to do them."

"What did you do?" Isla asked.

Josh replied, "A couple of things actually. Abby suggested doing a High Performance Pattern assessment with Mary Elizabeth to coach her around how she sees her strengths and skills fit her position at this time."

"She responded really well," Abigail said. "Turns out that right now she performs better as an account manager, growing relationships with our partners, rather than an account executive, starting new relationships."

"So once that was determined," Josh said, "we shifted her responsibilities, and she's at peak performance. Much happier and satisfied. Completely engaged."

Harper asked, "What was the second thing you did?"

"Abby suggested I ask how I could support her," Josh added. "And to pray for her. What I discovered is that since her husband left her with two preschoolers, Mary Elizabeth is stressed to the max. Like any of us would be. She just doesn't have energy to start those new account relationships."

"And what else did you do, Josh?" Abigail inquired.

"Well, I wasn't going to mention that," Josh said.

Abigail said, "I will then. Josh and Mandy had Mary Elizabeth's two preschool girls over for a sleepover one night so she could get dressed up and go out with some girlfriends. Josh even taught the older one to swim!"

"Oh my, Josh!" Isla exclaimed.

"And my understanding from Mary Elizabeth is the girls want to come back for more with Aunt Mandy and Uncle Josh," Abigail added.

Harper said, "That's amazing, Josh."

"Well, you know it wasn't us doing it," Josh said. "It was Christ in us. But we sure did have a great time! And Mary Elizabeth told Mandy that her husband left right after she miscarried an unexpected pregnancy."

Abigail said, "Oh my, now that's so hard."

"It really is a double indemnity," Josh replied, "which made Mary Elizabeth's night out more significant. And we had such an amazing experience, Mandy and I decided to start trying for our own kids after the wedding."

Harper replied, "And so it begins."

"Your God talk," Isla said, "is supported by God acts. Your intention took action. You're a role model for all of us, Josh."

Consider How God Nods at You

Read James 2:14–17. Think of a coworker you've talked to about what they "ought to do" and have yet to show them Christ's love. How can you "show" rather than just "tell" them about your faith?

The Thursday morning meeting was Isla's to lead. "Before we start on the fourth lie today, I want to thank each of you for letting me participate," she said. "I'm humbled to learn more about Jesus from you."

"The privilege is ours," Abigail said.

Isla responded, "Well, maybe," and smiled. "But I want you to know that I am so enjoying getting to know Jesus the way Mother did. I know he is present with me daily, and I'm confident we will achieve this breakthrough. I pray for Akorfa daily."

"She's making great progress," Harper added. "She's in the final stages of testing and is almost ready for human trials."

Josh said, "We're all here because each of us gave attention to God Nods."

"I believe that. And as we break these lies," Isla said, "I believe we shall save many, many lives. I just hope my daddy's is one of them."

Harper reached out and touched Isla's right hand. Their fingers curled around each other's until Lemondrop, who came to work with Josh again, walked over and put her head in Isla's lap and stared up at her. Her large, greenish eyes shared love.

"Oh Lemondrop, you are the best friend ever," Isla said.

Harper replied, "So what am I?" And the group laughed wildly. Lemondrop moaned.

As the laughter settled, Isla said, "The fourth lie is if you love God, you can hate another person, taken from 1 John 4:20–21."

"You know, if you read those two verses in the Amplified Bible, you discover that not only do you have to move from hate to love of the other person, but you must also "seek the best for him [or her]," Abigail said. "Sure is a lot easier just to hate them and move on. And yet that's not enough."

"More is required," Isla said. "I am grateful that you guys didn't hate me and move on, even though I'm sure I deserved it."

Harper said, "Well, we are, too, Isla. Just look at how much we'd have missed in knowing you better."

"Oh yes," Josh said, "had I stopped short at hating Mary Elizabeth and wanting to fire her, just think about how much harder life would have been for her. Abby helped me want the best and work for the best for her. And now look at her thriving. Leading her is easy now!"

Abigail joined in, "You know, we do miss so much when we dismiss others so quickly. Loving them and wanting the best for them means T2 grows more mature and achieves its mission better."

Isla raised her right hand and scratched behind Lemondrop's left ear and said, "And you know that may be the greatest treasure of all. To see Christ in others who are challenging to love and yet to love them anyway, even to want the best for them."

Her words wrapped around the minds of Abigail, Harper, and Josh in such a powerful embrace that their hearts were touched, too. They each sat watching Isla scratch behind Lemondrop's ear, a smile of pleasure slowly turning up her mouth. Lemondrop stuck her tongue out just a bit and groaned in delight.

Consider How God Nods at You

Read 1 John 4:20–21 in the Amplified Bible. Ask the Holy Spirit to bring to your mind one coworker whom you can love better, even want the best for, that you currently hate or at least strongly dislike. Name one action you can take to show love to this person. When will you do it? List three ways the company you both work for will benefit.

By the Friday morning gathering, the final one about the "5 Lies that Stop Your Action," the team saw more clearly the picture of how these lies inhibited breakthroughs like the nanoid sequence coding. As well, they had a new, fresh vision for how the truth debunking each lie would accelerate the breakthrough. Already they each claimed their identity in Christ more strongly. They thought of everyone as God's favorites. They were accountability partners to ensure consistency in their walk and talk. And they actively sought to work for the best of all the T2 teams, especially those difficult to love teammates.

Abigail began their final session with a prayer of gratitude, inviting Jesus to be present, and then said, "The fifth lie is, if others deserve your hatred, then it's justified, based on Matthew 5:43–47."

"The real enlightenment for me," Isla started, "was this notion of 'What have you really done if you only love those who love you?' That's the Campbell translation, by the way."

The quartet laughed, and then Harper said, "I like it and you know, that reality stopped me short, too. It's no secret I wish I could code people like nanoids to get them to do what I want them to do, especially Noah." She stopped to laugh at herself and then continued, "But you know, it's not my image breathed into them. It's God's image and likeness created in them. And so there must be a reason for that—a creative intentionality baked into all of us just like the antigens in our white blood cells that can cure most any disease, or so we believe."

The silence grew louder, and the only sound was Lemondrop's rhythmic snoring as each person weighed the truth of Harper's words.

She then said, "I'm not God, and when I try to justify my hatred of someone, I'm hating one of God's children. I can't live with that, no matter what someone else does to me."

Lemondrop rolled over and exhaled loudly.

After what seemed like an eternity, Josh spoke up. Lemondrop lifted her head at the sound of his voice. "Harper, it sounds like God already coded us for fellowship with one another and with Jesus. We just need Jesus to redeem us from within, to release grace in us, which we share with one another, regardless of behavior."

Isla jumped up from her chair and startled the quartet. Lemondrop barked her surprise. "That's it!" Isla screamed. "Sorry, girl," she said to Lemondrop. "I must call Akorfa right now." And with that she was out the door, turned right, and ran down the hall.

Lemondrop followed her, running close behind.

Consider How God Nods at You

Read Matthew 5:43–47. Who are you trying to code? And why? How did God already code this person? What is it about her/his behavior that makes it so challenging for you to love them?

Get the course, *The 5 Lies that Stop Your Action*, **when you subscribe to God Nods Resources here.**

Chapter 28

THE PRESENCE

sla sat beside her daddy as he reclined in his favorite chair in his home office. His light, peaceful breathing masked the battle within. "How are you today, Daddy?" she said softly.

"Oh, I didn't hear you come in," Elijah managed, startled. And with a slight smile said, "How long have you been staring at me, my brilliant daughter?" His dark eyes searched hers, found her best self, and embraced it.

She always loved her daddy's eyes.

"I just walked in, silly man," she said. "Just in time to catch you asleep on the job again. Whatever will I do with you?"

"I'm incorrigible," he chuckled. "I suppose you'll have to fire me."

To which Isla said, "If only I could."

She inhaled slowly and deeply, exhaled a quick prayer, and said, "Daddy, I have a couple of items to share with you if you're up to it."

"Of course I am," Elijah said, lifting himself weakly on his elbows, as if repositioning in his chair made him look larger. "Even more so if you'd make me a flat white."

"Anything for you, dear Daddy," Isla said as she kissed his forehead and moved to the coffee bar. "May I talk while I prepare it?"

"Not while you're steaming the milk," Elijah said. "You know I like mine extra hot."

"Well then, there's that," Isla said. She measured the espresso and made it while waiting for the macadamia nut milk to steam up. Her daddy was as specific about his flat whites as he was about his nanoid and antigen research. *What a pleasure to make him this drink*, she thought. *I sure hope I get to continue making them for him for a long time yet.*

She finished the flat white and turned back toward him. "And in your favorite mug," she said. The mug featured an oversized "T2" on one side and the other side, the one facing the drinker, read, "Discover the treasure within."

As Isla carefully handed her daddy the flat white, she looked behind him and up at the home office wall. "Daddy," she said, "how long has this quote from your father been on this wall?"

"Oh that's a recent addition," Elijah said matter-of-factly. "As I meditated one day, I remembered my father's final words to me. His face glowed when he said it like he was here, but not all of him. His eyes stared off as if he saw something no one else could."

"But Daddy," Isla said, "why didn't you tell me about this?"

"I'm telling you now, Isla," Elijah replied, "because you must be ready to know."

"Know what?" she said, her eyes scrolling over each twist and turn of the beautifully drawn, calligraphy-style letters.

"That," Elijah said and pointed to the wall.

Isla could contain her tears no longer, their hot streaks streamed down her cheeks, and fell on her daddy's lap. The same lap she sat in as a young girl to put her head on his chest and hear his heartbeat. The same lap she had longed to crawl up in when her mother died.

On the wall were these words: "Discover the treasure of God's presence within."

She sat down on the arm of the recliner, laid across her Daddy, carefully placing her weight on the other chair arm. She put her head on his chest and cried some more. His heartbeat was faint at first, then grew stronger.

Elijah patted her back with his left hand and carefully placed his flat white on the adjacent table with his right. Then with his right arm, he embraced her. And cried with her.

After a few moments, Elijah whispered, "Akorfa messaged me." Isla sobbed more loudly now.

The treasure within, God's presence, was discovered.

Consider How God Nods at You

Read John 11:35. Would Jesus have wept with Isla and Elijah? Why or why not?

Chapter 29

THE MOMENT

E lijah sat quietly, even pensively, as if what he was about to say held its own gravity. He stared off until Charlotte said, "Elijah, where is your attention right now?"

"Oh yes," Elijah said as if startled from a dream. "Where is my attention right now? Sure, Charlotte." And he fell silent again, his words trailing off. Then as he looked up, Charlotte sensed once again his deep searching of her soul through her eyes, discovering her best self, and lifting it up and out again as he smiled that wisp of a Mona Lisa smile.

And with that quick glance, which lasted an eternity for Charlotte, Elijah said, "I have something important to tell you. Something unlike anything you've heard before."

Consider How God Nods at You

Read Ephesians 5:15–16. Elijah was very careful, contemplating what to share with Charlotte and when. How do you recognize opportunities to share Jesus? What  criteria can you use to determine between wise and foolish sharing choices at work?

Chapter 30
THE BAPTISMS

"I can't believe this day is finally here!" Mandy said out loud to no one in particular and everyone in general. Lemondrop barked her excitement, ran toward the pool, and dove in with a splash so large that all the brunch group received a little sprinkle.

"Lemondrop wants to get baptized first," Josh shouted to the roaring laughter of the group. Even Isla and Elijah stopped their conversation and chuckled at the yellow Lab swimming around the pool, her head held high, as Mandy called her out.

"Baptism?" Elijah asked Isla who smiled.

"Yes, Daddy," she said. "You see, Jesus is the treasure within that your father talked about. He was baptized as an affirmation of his calling to set an example for us. It's an outer expression of an inner experience."

"How is that possible? That God came here from heaven as Jesus?" Elijah asked.

Isla caught his gaze and focused her eyes into his soul. "I don't know, Daddy. There are some realities that we discover rather than understand. Like the white blood cell antigens that cure diseases. Who knew they existed, much less how?"

"That's why my father said 'discover' instead of 'understand' the treasure within. And that's where the faith you talked about earlier enters," Elijah said. "Just like Akorfa tested and retested the sequencing. Only in faith do we administer to a person."

"Exactly," Isla said. She paused with her head down, listened as Mandy got Lemondrop out of the pool, and lifted her eyes to see into her daddy's again and said, "Jesus is the presence of God Mother talked to each morning. She planned to introduce me to him the day she died."

"So that's why you kept asking me who this Jesus is," Elijah said. "I had no idea, Isla. I am so sorry."

"I'm fine now, Daddy," Isla replied. "It's been a long time coming, in some ways a lifetime, but these incredible people you attracted to our team—Abigail, Harper, Josh—they have followed the God Nods to me and helped me see for the first time the true nature of our work."

"God Nods?" Elijah asked.

"Yes, God Nods," Isla said, "the unexpected and unexplainable convergence of abundant resources in a fullness of time that seems miraculous to us and yet is actually God helping us find the way."

Consider How God Nods at You

Matthew 6:33 in *The Message* says, "Steep your life in God-reality, God-initiative, God-provisions." Read Isla's definition of God Nods again. What does this definition mean to you? What's a God Nod you've experienced while reading this book? Or since reading this book?

"So Jesus is the presence of God who releases grace within us and heals our spirits, just like white blood cell antigens heal our bodies? He is like the nanoid, coded to win our battle within for us?" Elijah asked.

"Yes, exactly," Isla said.

"Why hasn't anyone ever told me about this Jesus before?" Elijah said.

"Well, from what I read on your wall, your father tried," Isla said.

"I always wondered what he meant. I knew there had to be more," Elijah confessed. "He died before I could ask him. Those were his final words, you know."

"And Daddy, I'm sure Mother tried," Isla offered.

Elijah dropped his head, ashamed. Finally, he said as if hearing it for the first time himself, "Yes, she did. More than you know. I have replayed so many of her words in my mind, especially during this battle with pancreatic cancer. She's the one who reminded me constantly that our T2 mission statement was incomplete. That I must add Father's words, 'of God's presence.' And yet because I didn't understand them, I failed to do so. Oh Isla, please forgive me."

Just then from the pool, Pastor Evangeline said, "If I may please have your attention, your full attention here?" Lemondrop whined to join her. Mandy held her leash firmly.

Isla whispered, "Of course, Daddy, anything for you" as she turned her chair toward the pool. Elijah shook his head in amazement, and wished Sophie was by his side again. She would be so pleased. And his father! What would he say now?

Pastor Evangeline continued, "Thank you so much for joining Mandy and Josh for this happy occasion of their wedding today *and* for their baptisms."

"Woo-hoo!" Harper yelled. Lemondrop barked in excitement, wagging her wet tail against Mandy's leg.

Pastor Evangeline continued, "Mandy and Josh, will you please join me in the pool?"

"Somebody's got to hold Lemondrop," Mandy said to everyone's delight.

Noah jumped up. "I'll take her," he said, and grabbed the leash. As he walked her over to their table, she paused beside Harper, and shook from head to tail.

"Oh my!" Harper shouted and again, and everyone laughed, especially Ernie.

"Well, this is a joyous occasion, and Lemondrop celebrates with us," Pastor Evangeline said. "The significance of today is joyous and meaningful. Mandy and Josh found each other in God's providence, which they will celebrate this afternoon. Jesus found Mandy and Josh with God's loving grace, which they celebrate now through baptism."

Isla moved up to the edge of her chair.

"Mandy," Pastor Evangeline said, "share with our friends who Jesus is to you."

Mandy paused to breathe. She looked deeply into Josh's eyes as he flashed his signature smile back at her.

"Jesus," Mandy said, "is the lover of my soul. It's taken me quite a while to say that out loud. If you know my story, you know what I mean."

Abigail smiled and nodded.

"This means," Mandy said, "that no matter where I've been or what I've done—good, bad, or indifferent—I am loved. I am worthy of Jesus's love. This love carries a grace with it that erases my bad and indifferent behavior, my sins, and celebrates the good. I fully receive this love of Jesus today because this love is reflected in my love for this man here." She took Josh's hand underwater and squeezed it. Lemondrop barked.

Elijah noticed Isla on the edge of her chair. She hung on every word Mandy said. He wondered what she was thinking but decided not to interrupt her. Instead, he moved forward in his chair. He leaned heavily on the table with his elbows and noticed less pain than usual.

"And now Josh," Pastor Evangeline said turning to him, "share with our friends who Jesus is to you."

Josh squeezed Mandy's hand three times for "I love you" and began. "Jesus to me is the sunrise that lights my path all day. Jesus to me is the amazing work we do as T2 to 'discover the treasure within.' For you see, the treasure is God's presence, Jesus, who is within me and each of you and our business partners and the persons we help him cure. Dr. Campbell, I hope it's OK I said that." Josh laughed nervously and looked at Elijah.

Consider How God Nods at You

Read Matthew 16:13-17. Who is Jesus to you?

Every head in the brunch group swiveled to look at Elijah who sat stunned, unable to speak. Isla turned to look at him. The sun peeked out from behind a dark cloud at that exact moment and cast its rays on Elijah's corner of the patio. Its bright light filled the corner, illuminating him as if it were a spotlight and the patio a theater. As if on cue, Lemondrop slipped quietly away from Noah who had dropped her lead, walked over to Elijah and sat in front of him. Her green, soulful eyes stared at him as if he were the only one present. Finally, he turned his gaze into the sun, which blinded him of everything and everyone except Lemondrop who glistened as the sun's rays danced off her coat's waterdrops.

All were still.

Finally, Elijah reached out and patted Lemondrop's head. "Of course, Josh," he said with a new strength in his voice. "And please, call me Elijah."

Lemondrop lay down beside Elijah.

After a silent moment, Pastor Evangeline declared softly, even reverently, "Surely Jesus is here with us."

The group murmured their approval.

"So, let me ask you this," she continued, "who is Jesus to you?"

The question lingered in the clearing sky briefly, and then she motioned Mandy to stand on her right side in the pool and Josh on her left. "Mandy and Josh wish to be baptized together," she said as she placed her hands on their backs. "So I now baptize you, Mandy, my sister in Christ, and, Josh my brother in Christ, in the name of the God who created you uniquely, the Jesus who redeems you for eternity, and the Holy Spirit who guides you daily. Amen." She gently guided them both as they went down under the water, grasped each other's hands, lingered briefly and then stood together.

The brunch group stood and wildly cheered their approval. Lemondrop barked three times.

As the clapping faded, Isla stepped up toward the pool, unsure of why until she stood on its edge, looking down at Mandy, Josh, and Pastor Evangeline. Everyone in the group stared intently and waited to hear what Isla would say. She heard herself say, "Is there room for one more?"

Everyone sat down slowly. By now the sun completely flooded the patio. Each person felt its warmth. J. W. reached for his sunglasses. The slightest breeze rustled the knockout roses at the patio's edge. Their bright red and pink blooms waved.

Mandy and Josh stood in the pool, unable to utter a sound. Pastor Evangeline smiled and opened her mouth to speak but did not. Her smile grew wider as she saw what Isla could not.

Elijah walked up beside his daughter, took her right hand in his left, and wrapped each of his fingers around hers. She turned, startled to see Daddy next to her. He immersed her in his eyes, searched her soul, found her best, and celebrated it. He smiled and said, "And one more?"

"Oh Daddy," Isla said, as she turned and leaned on him so hard he staggered. J. W. jumped up and caught him before he fell into the pool.

"I've gotcha mate," he said casually and held Elijah until he was steady on his feet again, then moved silently back to his seat. Abigail reached for his hand and smiled.

By now the sun was blinding.

Pastor Evangeline raised her eyebrows and squinted over at Mandy and Josh as if to ask, "Are you OK with this?" Josh smiled at Mandy, who kissed him, and both nodded their approval. They stepped back slightly.

Pastor Evangeline, still unable to speak, nodded yes. She moved to help Elijah down into the water.

Elijah looked down and said, his voice loud and clear, "I'm fine now." As if to add emphasis, Isla said, "He's fine now." And the two, daddy and daughter, stepped down into the water together.

Consider How God Nods at You

Read Matthew 3:13-17. What do you know or remember of your baptism? Of what significance is your baptism to your work?

Chapter 31
THE ANNOUNCEMENT

"What a beautiful wedding," Sally said to Harper. "I don't know when I have seen a happier, more peaceful couple."

Noah agreed. "They're certainly well suited for each other. And this is such a lovely B&B, don't you think, Carl?"

"I'll say," Carl responded. "They swam in each other's eyes the whole ceremony. And who knew they got baptized this morning? Was that here in the B&B's pool?"

Harper and Noah smiled at each other. She reached for his hand, which he took gladly. "No," Noah said, "they have a pool at their home."

"Daddy!" Ernie shouted as he ran up to Noah. "They have a dog and her name is Lemondrop. She likes me. I know because she licked the cupcake off my hand." And with that, Ernie disappeared just as quickly as he had appeared.

Harper and Noah stared at each other, dumbfounded.

"Is everything all right?" Sally asked.

Neither responded and instead just stood there, with a "what just happened?" look on their faces.

"Harper. Noah," Carl said. "Can I get you two something to drink?"

"No, we're fine," Harper finally managed, to which Noah added, "It's OK, friend."

"Well, what then?" Sally demanded. "What just happened? Is Ernie allergic to dogs or something?"

"No, in fact he loves dogs. Even wants one, but Harper keeps saying no," Noah said quietly.

Still staring at Noah, Harper, "Well, I might say yes now."

Carl said, "OK, well if that's all."

Harper interrupted, "That's the first time Ernie has called Noah 'Daddy.' He's called me 'New Mama' for a few months now. But that's the first time he's called Noah 'Daddy.'"

Slowly, a smile crept over Noah's face, and his eyes danced lightly, stopping only to wink at Harper. "He's never really known a father. Just men that moved in and out of his mother's life. The only faint memory he has of a man known as 'daddy' beat him often."

"Poor little fellow," Sally said.

Carl said, "My dad wasn't exactly a model citizen either."

"If everyone would take their seats please," Abigail announced.

"Oh, she's got the mic now," Harper said. "This should be fun, right 'Daddy'?"

Noah smiled large, hugged Harper, and said, "Sure, New Mama."

"As it's customary for the best woman to make a few remarks," Abigail continued, "I'd like to do that now. After all, I am the best woman."

Harper groaned loudly. J. W. stood, cheered, and said, "Yes you are!"

Mandy looked around for Josh, found him talking with Mary Elizabeth and her two daughters, who were flower girls in the ceremony, grabbed his hand, and led him over to the head table where they sat.

"I first met Mandy when she hosted a dinner party in their lovely home," Abigail said. "Mandy had such a great time she had to leave before dessert."

Josh hung his head and nodded. Mandy shouted, "Aw, now come on girlfriend!"

Abigail smiled broadly and said, "But wait! There's more! The second time we were together, Harper and I took her to the Southern Ideal Home Show at Dortna Arena, where she sobbed and cried most of the time."

Everyone laughed out loud, especially Harper.

"Not that Mandy is the emotional type or anything like that. Little did she know, we were a ruse that day so Josh could have decorators and caterers in to dress up their home for his marriage proposal that night," Abigail said.

"When she cried even more!" Josh yelled.

"And then there's Josh," Abigail said, "whom I almost didn't hire because he mistook Harper for me."

"Hey now, friend!" Harper said loudly.

"But when I told him that I was the nice one," Abigail continued, "he immediately agreed and understood so I hired him anyway."

Ernie slid over, got in Harper's lap, and said with a big grin, "I love you, New Mama, and I think you're nice. May I have a dog like Lemondrop? Please? She's going to have puppies."

"So as you can see," Abigail said, "Mandy and Josh are perfectly suited for each other. She is beautiful and brilliant in every way, and Josh is a great judge of character." And the crowd roared its approval. Lemondrop barked three times.

"Please New Mama? I'll take really good care of him, and you won't have to do a thing," Ernie pleaded.

"But the most important thing of all about this phenomenal couple is that while they are a match made in heaven, and love each other more than life, they love Jesus most of all," Abigail said.

And with that Elijah jumped out of his chair, shouted, "Here! Here!" and started clapping loudly. The rest of the reception crowd joined him, standing and clapping.

"So join me in raising a glass to this fine couple," Abigail said. "Here's to good health, good happiness, and a good God!"

As everyone sipped their champagne, Abigail said, "Now if you'll have a seat again, Akorfa and her husband have traveled all the way from Ghana to be here for this joyous celebration today."

"And baby Nathan, too!" Akorfa shouted, and her husband stood and held up the sleeping infant, his big smile one that only a new father can have.

"And baby Nathan, too!" Abigail repeated. "Akorfa has an announcement to make. Mandy's family and Kittrell Heights teachers, you're about to discover why you had to sign an

NDA to attend this wedding today!" Two tables of Mandy's colleagues raised their glasses. Five tables of Mandy's family members shouted, "Woo-hoo!" and one even hollered, "Roll Tide!"

Mandy, embarrassed, leaned over to Josh and said, "That's Uncle Bubba's son, Lil Bubba. Should I yell 'War Eagles'?"

"It's OK, sweetheart," Josh assured her. "They're just having fun."

Mandy leaned more on Josh, scooted her chair closer, kissed him, and said, "I sure do love you."

Akorfa took the microphone from Abigail and said, "Thank you, Abigail. I am pleased to announce officially for the first time that the final test results from our pancreatic cancer research are in. The final phase, which I have exhaustively tested and retested is back. The one phase we lacked, the self-destruct sequence, now works flawlessly. To God be the glory!"

The entire crowd leaped to their feet, roaring their approval. Even Lil Bubba jumped up. Lemondrop barked and barked and chased her tail until she spotted Ernie and ran to him.

Isla stood and clapped loudly, tears streaming down her cheeks onto her gown. She didn't mind crying now. Transparently. Loudly. Before God and everyone there. For these were tears of joy, a far different kind of tears than grief. Isla felt freer than she had since she was fifteen.

Now her daddy stood a chance of winning his battle. The taonga would be his! She turned to speak her hope to him, when Akorfa spoke again.

"Friends," Akorfa said, "I have one more important bit of news. The FDA has already given its initial approval."

While the crowd roared its joy even louder this time, Isla turned quickly around to her daddy, and said, "But how could they without human trials?"

Elijah smiled and stared into her questioning eyes. Before he could answer, Akorfa announced, "Because our founder, Dr. Elijah Campbell, was the first human trial. He tested the nanoid infusion on himself, and we're pleased to announce he is now in remission from his pancreatic cancer!"

"Why didn't you tell me?" Isla yelled at Elijah, hardly able to believe what she just heard. "Is it really true?"

"Yes, brilliant daughter," Elijah said loudly in her right ear. "It is!"

"It's truly a miracle!" Isla shouted. She threw her arms around his neck, and they embraced, one of those hugs filled with hope and a future, a melding of two hearts that will spend today and eternity together.

"Indeed it is," Elijah said. "And I have seen two more miracles here today. Jesus loves us."

"Oh Daddy, yes he does!" Isla said.

Mandy stared deeply into Josh's eyes. He returned her gaze with an intensity that only divine love births. They kissed passionately.

Just then, having found the B&B's pool, Ernie and Lemondrop jumped in, the two best cannonballs you've ever seen.

The brunch group's laughter was so loud it rose to heavenly heights.

And God nodded.

Consider How God Nods at You

Read John 2:1–11. Jesus's first miracle was at a wedding celebration. When the disciples saw that he could change water to "the best wine," they put their faith in him.

What inhibits you from putting your faith in Jesus? What might happen at work to prompt you to place more faith in Jesus? How does Jesus's performing this miracle encourage you at work?

Chapter 32
THE SERVANT

Abigail, Harper, Josh, Isla, and Elijah sat together away from the crowd who danced to the band, their horn section blasting out Earth, Wind and Fire's "Shining Star."

"But Daddy," Isla said, "how could you keep this decision to yourself? You should have consulted with us."

The horn section played in the distance as the vocalist belted out again, "What you can truly be . . ."

"I didn't do it for myself," Elijah said. "I did it for you, Isla, and all of you and those around the world who have pancreatic cancer. I did it so you could learn and move the research forward, so you would discover the treasure of God's presence within."

The weight of his words settled on the quartet. Arguing with such an impeccably pure, spiritually focused answer was futile. Isla knew it and so did the rest of them.

"How are you feeling today?" Abigail asked.

Elijah smiled and said, "Thank you, Abby. I feel a little better each day. My doctors at Duke say it will take time for my body to heal. But my white blood cells are releasing the necessary antigens to destroy the cancer cells, and my pancreatic functions are increasing a little more each day."

The five of them sat basking in the glory of the moment.

"God is good," Harper said.

"All the time," Abigail replied.

"Oh, we need another chair," Josh said. "I'll get it" and he moved a sixth chair over from another table.

"Who's that for?" Elijah asked.

Isla smiled and replied, "It's for Jesus. Evidently he gets tired of standing."

Elijah's quizzical expression made them all laugh.

Lemondrop appeared suddenly, paused to bark as they laughed, and then shook pool water on the group. "New Mama," Ernie yelled. "We went swimming. You're not mad, are you?"

The group, now sprinkled a second time today, laughed long and hearty, drinking deeply of the moment's sweetness.

"Of course not, buddy," Harper said. "How could I be?"

Isla looked at her daddy and smiled deeply into his eyes.

"How could I be, indeed," she said.

Elijah returned her smile. And nodded.

Consider How God Nods at You

Read John 15:13. What are you willing to do for your company or coworker(s) that resembles your laying down your life?

Chapter 33
THE UNVEILING

Charlotte Wilson's pulse increased immediately.

This must be why he agreed to do this interview, she thought. *What important announcement could it be?*

The producer in her ear said, "OK kid, stay calm. Relax. Just ask the question."

Charlotte smiled nervously and in her most professional voice said, "And what is this something important, Elijah? Something unlike anything we've heard before?"

"Well, actually, there are two important matters," Elijah began. "The second was unknown even to me until just this week."

"And what could that be?" Charlotte asked, her calm exterior masked her racing heart.

"Just tell us!" the producer in her ear said.

"Most New Zealanders knew of my father and knew him to be a generous man," Elijah said.

"Yes," Charlotte replied, "his contributions to student scholarships at the University of Auckland and sponsorship of the Maori collection at Auckland Museum are well documented."

"And he took such great care of his teams. Well it turns out that there's more," Elijah said.

"Really?" Charlotte said. "What is this more?"

"I'm getting ahead of myself, Charlotte," Elijah said. "I must back up and first announce that our company, Taonga Technologies, has discovered the cure for pancreatic cancer using our patented process of coding nanoids to stimulate white blood cells to release antigens which kill the cancer cells and allow the body to heal. This is our first breakthrough into the disease of cancer, and we anticipate rapidly discovering more cures."

"Why Dr. Campbell! That's marvelous!" Charlotte exclaimed.

"Thank you, Charlotte," Elijah said. "It really is. I'm particularly grateful for this news as I was diagnosed with pancreatic cancer just six months ago and until two weeks ago was in stage 4 myself."

"What?" Charlotte said. "So you're living proof that the cure works!"

"Officially I'm just in remission, Charlotte," Elijah said, "but yes I should be cured within a matter of months, if not weeks."

"Well, that's just . . ." Charlotte searched for the right word.

"Miraculous?" Elijah offered.

"Certainly, thank you. Yes, miraculous," Charlotte stammered and then thought, *Okay, kid, it's not every day a billionaire entrepreneur with a PhD and an MD announces on your show that he's cured pancreatic cancer . . . and himself!*

The producer in her ear said, "Pull yourself together."

"Dr. Campbell, that's amazing news, and yet you mentioned you have two announcements to share," Charlotte recovered and said. "I take it this second one has something to do with your father, Oliver Campbell."

"That's right," Elijah said. "When I announced to the T2 board about our breakthrough to a cancer cure, right after the meeting, the attorney who administers my late father's estate asked to see me. Said it was important."

"Was it?" Charlotte asked and leaned forward in her chair.

"Turns out it was very important," Elijah said, "for all of us. Father's estate has released all of its assets to support our further cancer cure research contingent on the treatment being made available free to everyone who suffers from whatever cures we discover."

Charlotte sat stunned, unable to speak. Her producer said in her ear, "Charlotte, say something!" She could not so Elijah continued.

"The goal is to totally eradicate cancer of any kind anywhere on the planet and at no cost to the patients," he said.

"Ask him how large the estate is!" Charlotte's producer screamed in her ear.

"Um, Elijah, that's a remarkable gesture of generosity and a lofty goal," Charlotte managed to say. "If I may ask, just how large is Oliver Campbell's estate?"

Elijah paused and said, "Its current value is about $692.7 billion New Zealand dollars, which is about $500 billion in U.S. dollars, Charlotte."

Charlotte sat stunned again. "Charlotte, say something, anything," her producer yelled in her ear.

"Well," Charlotte said slowly, "that should provide a lot of free cancer treatment and research around the world, Dr. Campbell."

"It's Elijah," he said gently, "and yes it should. And yet I've thought of a third announcement I'd like to share with your viewers, Charlotte."

"You mean there's more?" Charlotte said without thinking.

Elijah chuckled to himself. "Yes, there is, and it's something my father left me that's even more valuable."

Once again, Charlotte couldn't speak.

"I got nothing," the producer in her ear said in exasperation.

"Me either," Charlotte said out loud, then recovered enough to smile and say, "Whatever could be more valuable than you cured pancreatic cancer, you're personally cured of pancreatic cancer, and a $692.7 billion bequest to eradicate cancer with free treatments internationally?"

Consider How God Nods at You

Read Matthew 25:14-30 in *The Message*. What could Jesus mean when he said, "It's criminal to live cautiously like that!" and refers to the third person as a "play-it-safe"? How did Oliver Campbell avoid this fate? How did his son Elijah avoid this same fate? How will you avoid it with your talents?

Chapter 34
THE WITHIN

"That's what I once thought, Charlotte," Elijah said. "Now I understand more fully what my Father meant."

"About what?" Charlotte asked, just trying to keep the conversation going.

Elijah laughed softly, his eyes dancing, yet stopping long enough to wink at Charlotte. She smiled nervously and thought, *Did he just wink at me?*

"When you asked me why I named this company Taonga Technologies, I told you what my father said to me so often as a young lad," Elijah said.

"Yes, he said that he had discovered great treasures from the earth, and he wanted you to discover great treasures within and tapped you on the chest," Charlotte replied.

Elijah said. "That's correct. That's what he said." Elijah paused to collect his thoughts. He knew he must say this just right. "Charlotte, I was with my father when he died from COVID-19. His death propelled me down the path I'm on today. However, only recently, his final words to me have sent me down another path, one more valuable."

"What did he say?" Charlotte asked softly, leaning forward in her chair, unable to control her interest.

Elijah smiled and suddenly saw himself back in Father's bedroom, sitting on the side of his bed, leaning over his frail, barely breathing body, with his ear to Father's mouth, straining to hear the whispering voice as it struggled to say those most important words.

"Elijah, what did he say?" Charlotte asked again, even more softly.

Elijah's eyes filled with tears as he relived the moment, so much more poignant now that he understood fully what Father meant. His own voice struggled to repeat those most important words. "His face glowed, Charlotte," Elijah began. "He stared beyond that room. It's as if he was in two places simultaneously. He said, 'Ah! Now I understand. Discover the treasure . . . of God's presence . . . within.'"

Charlotte sat quietly, immersed in the sanctity of the moment. She ignored the cameras, the producer screaming in her ear, "Say something, anything!" and instead entered the sacred space with Elijah. She reached for his hand, touched it lightly, and as he looked up, smiled at him. She understood in a way she never had before.

Later she would say how unexplainable the moment was and yet how it was more real than any previous moment in her life.

"You see," Elijah continued, "the greatest treasure of all is within each of us. It's God's presence. This presence is what unites us as humans despite our differences. God's image and likeness are in all of us, only we distort the beautiful treasure our Creator places within. So God came here in Jesus to do for what us what we can't do for ourselves."

Charlotte asked, "And what is that Elijah?"

"Jesus redeems us, releases loving grace within us," Elijah said, "just like the nanoids prompt white blood cells to release antigens that destroy cancer cells."

The producer stopped screaming. The camera operators stepped from behind their lenses. And for just a moment, one sacred, ordained moment, they all, Charlotte included, nodded.

"So we have everything we need within," Charlotte said, a Mona Lisa wisp of a smile emerging across her lips as she spoke, "we just need Jesus to redeem and release our best, loving gracious selves."

"That's it, Charlotte," Elijah exclaimed, amazed at how quickly she understood.

Charlotte's smile grew smaller as she remembered the many times she was less than her best self—the way she treated the producer in her ear and the camera operators as beneath her, how she assumed her boyfriend could rearrange his life for her every whim, and the disdain with which she regarded her fans who gathered outside the studios after every morning's show.

"We just need Jesus to redeem and release our best, loving gracious selves," Elijah repeated her words.

"But how do we do that?" Charlotte asked so honestly that the production crew gasped because that's what they wondered, too.

"Thanks for that question," Elijah said. "I have found in the last week that it's far simpler and easier than I imagined. It begins with your accepting that God's presence is in you."

"I see that now," Charlotte said.

The producer in her ear said, "I do, too."

"Then you next accept the gift of Jesus's help to redeem your best efforts and help you do what you can't do for yourself—release your best self to work and live daily," Elijah said.

"Well if Jesus is God's presence, and God's image and likeness are in here," Charlotte said as she placed her hand on her heart, "then yes, I know I need help being my best self."

She paused, hand on heart, hoping against hope that her past did not disqualify her from redemption. She blurted out, in desperation, "Can Jesus help even me?"

And with that Charlotte, despite the cameras and everything that went with them, released her tears of pent-up frustration, insecurity, and lack of ever feeling quite good enough. The scars of all of her battles within, especially those with the producer in her ear, began to release. The wounds started to heal. She felt different within, her heart strangely warmed.

Elijah smiled at Charlotte as he watched her countenance transform. She held her head up now. Her smile returned. Her eyes danced, stopping only to wink—yes, wink—at Elijah. He knew her question was answered. Jesus could help even her. She had discovered the most valuable treasure of all—the presence of God within.

"I understand now," she finally said, "why this third announcement is the most valuable of all."

The producer in her ear said, "Me, too."

And all the camera operators nodded.

Consider How God Nods at You

Read Acts 9:3-18. What is most valuable to you about this announcement? What in your past can Jesus redeem?

Chapter 35
THE FINALE

The cheers were deafening.

Louder than summer thunder from a lightning strike six feet away.

And in some ways, that's what happened.

Lightning struck.

More than twice.

There really is more rejoicing in heaven over one person's redemption than anything else in all creation.

"I love it when this happens," Sophie Campbell said.

"It really is unlike anything on earth," Oliver Campbell agreed. "It took quite a while for me to get used to it."

"I don't think I'll ever grow accustomed to it," Sophie replied. "It's unique every time."

"I know what you mean," Oliver said. "And this one is particularly unique."

"Yes, it really is," Sophie said, nodding her head in agreement. "And especially meaningful, too."

"Who knew God would choose to employ my Elijah in such a powerful, transforming manner?" Oliver asked.

"I saw such within him throughout my life," Sophie said, "I just wasn't sure if he . . ."

"I know what you mean," Oliver said. "I suppose we both lacked faith. I understand better now how God works all things together for good," Oliver confessed. "I wished I had realized sooner what the most valuable treasure within was all about. All of this would have happened much earlier if I had told Elijah."

"Yes," Sophie added, "I had a similar wish that I had shared more about Jesus earlier with Isla. Had I only known that day would be my last on earth." Her voice trailed off like a cloud pushed by the wind.

"And yet all things in life really do work together for good," Oliver said.

"We just had to trust God to work it out," Sophie said.

The angelic cheering grew louder now as TVNZ aired Charlotte's interview of Elijah. New Zealanders nodded within to recognize God's presence, one after another—then more and more as the word spread of additional cancer cures and free treatments.

And the word spread of the source of all of this loving grace, the greatest treasure of God's presence within—taonga.

And then, just when Oliver and Sophie assumed the cheering would ease, it only grew louder, exponentially so, as Charlotte's interview went viral in Africa, Europe, South America, and finally the U.S. Each time the celebration rose higher and higher.

"And Isla? What about her growing influence?" Oliver asked.

Sophie said, "Oh yes, my goodness. Her brilliance grows daily. She was always such a curious child and intuitive, too. She now matures into her full potential with God's help."

"Once she discovered that greatest treasure within was God's presence, Jesus became very personal with her," Oliver said. "I celebrate their closeness. It's a rare intimacy."

Oliver and Sophie yelled to be heard now. The angelic celebration grew more deafening as a multitude of persons, one by one, accepted God's presence within and Jesus as the one who released loving grace within them. Even by heaven's infinite standards, this party was loud.

Soon even their loudest voices grew too dim to be heard as the rejoicing grew to a cosmic-sized symphony of delight. Sophie and Oliver could only smile . . . and nod.

Consider How God Nods at You

Read Acts 10. Peter released his limiting beliefs and became vulnerable in order to share Jesus with Cornelius. His greatest challenge was obedience to sharing with Cornelius. What is your greatest barrier to sharing Jesus? What is a first step to overcoming it? What support do you need?

Their smiles grew wider, consuming their entire selves as the angels began singing: "Hallelujah! Hallelujah! Hallelujah!"

"Ah!" Sophie mouthed to Oliver. "It's 'The Chorus'!"

They both reveled in the sheer joy of the moment. Wave after wave of love washed over the entire cosmos as the faith of more and more people focused on a personal relationship with Jesus.

It was like an earthquake rumbling through heaven as the angels' final Hallelujah! erupted. It rang down the halls of eternity, redeeming errant actions and unintended consequences for generations past, present, and future.

Sophie and Oliver and everyone else in heaven were perfectly still, listening to the last note's reverberation. Then God's still, small voice whispered, "So let it be."

While a whisper, this divine still, small voice called out to everyone on earth.

Lemondrop's puppy, Lemonade, barked three times.

"What is it boy?" Ernie asked. "New Mama, Daddy, Lemonade's barking at something."

"I thought I heard something, too," Harper said to Noah who then said, "Hey Ernie, listen carefully. Dogs have better hearing than we do."

Oliver and Sophie smiled.

And God nodded.

Consider How God Nods at You

Read 1 Kings 19:9-13. Share an experience when you heard God's still, small voice calling out to you. How did you initially react? What action did you take after deciding it was God's voice? How did your action affect your coworkers?

"And let the loveliness of our Lord, our God, rest on us, confirming the work that we do. Oh, yes. Affirm the work that we do!" (Psalm 90:17)

ACKNOWLEDGMENTS

Morgan James Publishing took us in when we were ready to give up on publishers. Bonnie, David, Jim, Amber, and a holy host of others that now includes Tom Dean are simply the finest on the planet at what they do. Publishing with you guys is like doing stand-up comedy. You find a way to say yes! Thanks MJP for following the God Nods.

Jane Creswell: I've felt God called me to be a missionary to the corporate world since my college days. Some key people inspired me to stay the course of this unconventional calling. My fourth-grade Bible Drill coach, Edith Crawford, taught me my journey would be only as sure-footed as the care I gave to seeking application of the passages found throughout my Bible. My college pastor, Dr. John Jeffers, taught me that I should be as diligent in pursuing God's purpose for my vocation as I was in my pursuit of a college degree. And my self-appointed mentor during my summer missions experience, Charles Creswell (who later became my father-in-law), taught me to treat everyone at work as someone Jesus loved so much he died for their redemption. Each of these folks is already celebrating eternity in heaven, and yet their influence lives on in me and hopefully also those I'm called to love. I'm grateful to my family for their support and most especially, Tom, my true love, for always being there for me on my Jesus-crazy adventures.

And I'm forever grateful for Dr. Joey Faucette, my brother in Christ and partner in ministry, as we serve the organizations and coaches God puts before us. Thanks for making this book come alive with a compelling story line and characters that jump off the page and into our hearts. I look forward to many more Jesus-crazy adventures ahead!

Joey Faucette: My wife and best friend, Rowan, read this early on and drew straight lines from these characters to people I know. She's right. All writing is autobiographical. So thanking everyone is impossible. I begin with her as she, second only to Jesus, is primary in all I do.

Viola Babcock and Dorothy Whitley shaped this backwater, Eastern North Carolina, aspiring writer into someone whose work others want to read . . . someone besides his mother who reads it all regardless. There may be a little of each of them in Harper.

Charlotte Forrest impressed upon me early the importance to "study to show thyself approved." She would have loved Elijah and Isla Campbell.

Archie Mosley set the bar high in being a Jesus follower, and I still sniff his trail rambling through my heart. Abigail sounds a lot like him.

Jane Creswell is the sister I hoped for that my daddy never told me about. It's challenging to find someone Jesus crazy and yet terra firma focused to collaborate with me. I get that. And I get you. I am grateful!

DANVILLE PITTSYLVANIA CANCER ASSOCIATION

We gift a percentage of this book's retail price to
the Danville Pittsylvania Cancer Association, a hometown
nonprofit in Virginia that provides patient support.
Join us in supporting this amazing cause!

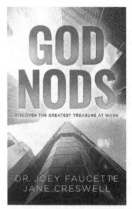

Join Abigail, Harper, Josh, Isla and other Jesus-followers around the world who discover the greatest treasure at work—their faith—through God Nods Resources. This online resource includes:

Three virtual courses: *7 Keys to More God Nods*, *Be Still and Know*, and *The 5 Lies That Stop Action*.

A weekly brief video with activities that increase your faith with greater joy so you love God and others more. You watch the video, do the activities, and then discuss in a fellowship of fellow believers that you create or join virtually or in-person.

A 20-minute midweek, virtual God Nod worship experience in which you pray in breakout rooms with other Jesus-followers about faith and work.

A quarterly God Nod Zoom Party with the authors, Joey Faucette and Jane Creswell, in which you share your God Nod experiences at work, ask questions, and have fun with faith at work!

Scan this QR code to discover more and join today:

A free ebook edition is available with the purchase of this book.

To claim your free ebook edition:

1. Visit MorganJamesBOGO.com
2. Sign your name CLEARLY in the space
3. Complete the form and submit a photo of the entire copyright page
4. You or your friend can download the ebook to your preferred device

Print & Digital Together Forever.

Snap a photo

Free ebook

Read anywhere